Putting Difference to Work

By the same author

Patterns of Brief Family Therapy

Keys to Solution in Brief Therapy

Clues: Investigating Solutions in Brief Therapy

A NORTON PROFESSIONAL BOOK

Putting Difference to Work

Steve de Shazer
Brief Family Therapy Center
Milwaukee, Wisconsin

W. W. NORTON & COMPANY • *NEW YORK* • *LONDON*

Library of Congress Cataloging-in-Publication Data
De Shazer, Steve.
    Putting difference to work / Steve de Shazer.
        p.   cm.
    Includes bibliographical references.
    ISBN 0-393-70110-7
    1. Family psychotherapy.   2. Brief psychotherapy.   3. Family
psychotherapy – Case studies.   4. Brief psychotherapy – Case studies.
I. Title.
    [DNLM: 1. Family Therapy.   2. Psychotherapy, Brief.   QM 430.5
D456p]
RC488.5.D43   1991   616.89′156 – dc20   90-14185

W. W. Norton & Company, Inc., 500 Fifth Avenue, New York, N.Y. 10110
W. W. Norton & Company, Ltd., 10 Coptic Street, London WC1A 1PU

1 2 3 4 5 6 7 8 9 0

FOREWORD

Helm Stierlin

In a footnote to one of this book's later chapters, Steve de Shazer refers to his simplemindedness. He apologizes for it, fearing he might do injustice to the philosophers he quotes and uses, particularly Wittgenstein and Derrida.

But what he calls his simplemindedness represents, in my view, his perhaps greatest asset and strength. It reflects qualities that allow him to take a fresh look at things, to be concise and to the point, to be a pragmatist in the best sense of the term, and to not be awed by what authorities have thought and taught before him. In brief, it allows him to be original and innovative.

These qualities mark his work as a therapist. They account for the worldwide success of the kind of brief solution oriented therapy that he pioneered. They also mark the work that he presents in this volume – intellectual, if you wish, philosophical work – that takes up the theory of therapy and, particularly, the theory of brief therapy. There is the same freshness, the same emphasis on what works and on what makes sense that characterizes his writings on the more pragmatic aspects of therapy. However, this does not mean he skirts complexity. Rather, he manages to reduce complexity in a way that keeps complexity in sight of the reader and keeps the access to it open. In this volume, this can be seen in how he deals with intricate semiotic and semantic issues, yet does so with concern for conceptual clarity, preciseness, and a grasp of what is essential.

I believe the implications of his investigations are far-reaching. Perhaps most important, he makes a convincing case for the fact that brief therapy – i.e., a therapy lasting no longer than ten sessions, but often much less – is not only a second-best substitute for a lengthy dynamic therapy but often is the very best that a client can get. This follows from his exposition of therapy as a special form of a language game. In this exposition, old shibboleths depicting therapy as a kind of archaeological excavation – be this tedious or heroic – carried out with or, perhaps more correctly, against a resisting client, cease to make sense. It is particularly the later writings of Wittgenstein and of post-structuralist thinkers such as Derrida and de Man which allow Steve de Shazer to make his case, i.e., the case for therapy as a "negotiated, consensual, and cooperative endeavor in which the solution-focused therapist and client jointly produce various language games focused on a) exceptions, b) goals, and c) solutions."

At the end of the book, Steve de Shazer muses whether this exercise in interactional constructivism may not have been too radical, too shocking for some readers. This may be the case. But I could not help recalling a dictum of Nietzsche which happens to be one of my favorites: "A very popular error: Having the courage of one's convictions; rather it is a matter of having the courage for an attack on one's convictions." I consider it to be one of the great merits of this book that it invites us to muster the courage to attack our convictions.

FOREWORD

John H. Weakland

Putting Difference to Work is an unusual work, and not everyone should read it. This book examines family therapy (implicitly, all psychotherapy) broadly, and de Shazer's own solution-based brief therapy in particular, from the "outside." Its unusual subject is therapy as such, as observed conversation between client and therapist. Its unusual means involve using concepts from constructivism and post-structuralist textual analysis. One might call this a meta-therapy study, a work of inquiry aimed more at raising basic questions than at offering specific answers.

Obviously, then, this book is not for those who are happy with the state of the field of psychotherapy, their concepts, and their present methods of practice. Since de Shazer's work begins by suggesting strongly that we don't even know what we mean by "family therapy" and proceeds to propose that we need to think differently about the very nature of therapy if it is to be brief and effective, this book would probably only confuse and irritate such satisfied therapists.

Equally, it is not a work for those – a large number if we can judge from the nature of many books and workshops in the field – who are not satisfied but are looking for recipes, specific procedures to apply to what they see as specific and discrete types of problems. While this book presents and discusses a number of fascinating cases, it not only is not a therapy cookbook, but also questions the value of such cookbooks.

These two kinds of therapists—those who are satisfied with the status quo and those looking only for simple specific answers (often while taking complex and doubtful general premises for granted, however)—probably constitute a large majority of the profession. But this perhaps is only to be expected. We live in a time of conformity, and work in a field where there are considerable pressures from both our clients and our colleagues to act as if we know all the answers, although it seems evident enough that many of our answers do not work all that well.

Nevertheless, I believe, or at least hope, that there still exists a considerable number of therapists who should be interested in and should read this book. I think of two main kinds of potential readers: those who are serious enough about therapy and its potentials to be dissatisfied with the current state of thinking and practice, and those who are playful enough to be curious about where looking at our enterprise in new ways might lead. Of course, a given person might be both—for example, Steve de Shazer.

This foreword is obviously an endorsement of this book, at least for a certain audience. It is not an endorsement without reservation, however. While I found this work both stimulating and enlightening, there are a number of things in it with which I do not agree. Since this is a foreword and not a review, I will only give two examples here. At a specific level, I do not think that use of the term "strategy" necessarily implies a contest between therapist and client; indeed, I would propose that de Shazer carries on his therapeutic conversations strategically. More broadly, it seems to me that while he has made good use of ideas from the deconstructionists, some of his use of their terms could be misleading. To shift from the terminology of "reading" a text and "understanding" a client's messages to "misreading" and "misunderstanding" seems like jumping from the frying pan into a mirror-image frying pan. Does not "misreading" itself imply the existence of some "correct" reading, rather than simply saying that messages always and necessarily are *interpreted*?

I trust that stating such reservations will not detract from my endorsement, but rather support its credibility, since, despite my initial caveats, I think many people should read this book and read it thoughtfully.

CONTENTS

PREFACE

This book continues the trend, highly noticeable in my previous book (de Shazer, 1988), of looking at the therapeutic interview as a conversation. This is not a direction that I looked for or desired or even thought might be useful. It is as if this direction has been forced on me by my surroundings and I am just following along blindly.

Ever since my colleagues and I started to construct solutions, rather than solve problems, we have tried to show what it means when we say things like "You do not need to know what the problem is in order to solve it," or "The problem or complaint is not necessarily related to the solution," or "The solution is not necessarily related to the problem." These ideas about solutions, which we have been developing since 1982, were as strange to us at the beginning as they now are to some of the therapists who read about our work, come to our workshops and training programs, watch our videotapes, or watch us work "live."

Since 1982, my colleagues and I have been struggling with presenting our ideas in useful ways as we continue to work out the implications and ramifications of those ideas in our work with clients. It is our work with clients, of course, that continuously leads to our having to find new ways to describe what we and our clients do and new ways to analyze the clinical situation: We need these new ways simply because the old ways to describe and analyze, even our own old ways, refuse to work anymore.

In the summer of 1989 we had a case (see Chapters 6 and 7) that prompted descriptions that were apparently different from our previous types of descriptions. We saw something for the first time and our old descriptive tools were stretched to their limits; therefore, we had to do something different.

I felt as if I were forced into viewing interviews as if they were texts, stories, pieces of literature. This is exactly the direction I did not want to go because I was afraid that it would lead us away from the *pragmatics of doing brief therapy*.

For many years, I have been looking at philosophy, what might broadly be called the philosophy of language, and the sociology of knowledge (sort of a hobby of mine) and have considered most of that to be too abstruse to be of any use in the day-to-day work of brief therapists. But this particular case pointed to the potential usefulness of my hobby! What had been a minor or secondary form of description became, at least for now and at least for this book, a primary or major form of description.

The results of describing a particular case in a certain way, a way new for us, led to an unfamiliar way of looking at and describing solution-focused brief therapy. Along the way, I have had to redescribe a lot of territory I had previously covered and to look again at how these ideas about problems, complaints, exceptions, and goals connect with perhaps related ideas in the family therapy discourse and even in the larger psychotherapy discourse.

* * *

The way I present my views (as well as the perspective itself which is held to a greater or lesser extent by my colleagues) may be disquieting to a few, or even many, readers. Since I consider reading to be an interactive and creative endeavor, you, as readers, will sometimes be called upon to build links for yourself between sections of the book. I will suggest certain links, but I will leave others open to you. This will be the signal:

* * *

This means that a section is finished and a new section will begin. The connection between the two sections may sometimes be less than obvious and that is where creative reading comes in. I suspect that, at least in part, this rather indirect approach comes from my reading of Ludwig Wittgenstein and from Milton Erickson's indirect approach to therapy. At other points, the juxtapositions may be unmarked but nonetheless the link no more obvious. This writing technique is analogous to a technique in music where a particular sequence of notes can be *heard* to include notes that were not played. Jazz great Charlie Parker, for instance, could frequently be *heard* to play notes below the range of the alto sax. People transcribing his work, musicians who perhaps did not know the range of the instrument, would even write down those notes – notes that were not played and could not be played on the alto sax. (I played the alto sax for years and I, too, heard Charlie Parker play notes I could not play. He did a lot of things with the sax that I could never do.)

* * *

Actually, the ideas themselves may be even more disquieting than the forms I have chosen to use as a package. However, the ideas from the philosophy of language suggest ways of viewing our work that point to the differences between our assumptions and some of the assumptions common to the field. They also point to the implications of our view of the disconnectedness of problems and solutions and lead to descriptions that allow both client and therapist greater freedom in their work of developing solutions.

I hope that you, as readers, will have as much fun reading this book as I did writing it. At times the writing was very difficult, and so I assume that at times the reading of it will also be difficult. But, primarily, the work has been much more fun than any of my previous books. Perhaps it is just that here I play with ideas and with thinking about how to do therapy.

* * *

This book could not have been written without the support and encouragement of my colleagues Insoo Kim Berg, Wallace Gingerich, Ron Kral, Gale Miller (who read many of the versions of this work as it developed), and of course, our office manager Dolores Van Erden. Furthermore, this book owes a lot to the various people who have participated in our training programs at the Brief Family Therapy Center in Milwaukee and to the various people who have participated in my workshops and seminars. Without their questions, I would not have known about the answers and it is these questions and answers that make up the bulk of this book. Some sections of some chapters were begun in 1972 (see, in particular, material on the concept of causality), some sections come from unpublished and/or unfinished essays written during the course of the past 10 years, and some sections, particularly those framing therapy sessions as a set of language games rather than as one language game are based, in part, on a paper as yet unpublished in English, "Beyond Complaints" that I wrote with Gale Miller (Miller & de Shazer, 1991).

* * *

Over the past 20 years of doing, studying, and teaching about brief therapy, my work has been described as "pragmatic to the max," or so apparently simple – and perhaps even simplistic – that it is "minimalist to the max." Certainly the model of therapy that my colleagues and I have developed is relatively simple, although the associated thinking is not as apparently simple. I have been described as the "most minimal of the minimalists" and therefore as "using as few words as possible" in my therapy sessions and, in my workshops and books, as "giving as little explanation as possible."

> **explanation, 1:** the act of explaining, expounding, or interpreting; exposition; illustration; interpretation; the act of clearing from obscurity and making intelligible. **2:** that which makes clear. **3:** the sense given by one explaining it; interpretation; meaning.[1]

---

[1] Throughout, unless otherwise noted, these definitions are from *Webster's New Twentieth Century Dictionary, Unabridged Second Edition.*

I give descriptions of what happens in therapy, what therapists and clients *do together*, but people (i.e., therapists reading or attending training programs or workshops) want or seem to want an explanation of the kind that is common to the therapy world. In other words, their questions show that they want interpretation of, speculation about, and/or description of *causal* processes: the interpretation of something done in such a way that its parts or elements appear operationally connected to its generation. I, like Sadler and Hulgus (1989), "reserve 'explanation' for the description of *causal processes*, for example, those of physiology or chemistry. We [Sadler & Hulgus] use 'understanding' to describe human *meanings* and *not* causal processes" (p. 258). Further, I use "description" to refer to describing meaning or use, and reserve "understanding" or better, "misunderstanding" for a particular usage (see Chapter 6).

Frequently I have been told that my therapy sessions do not even *look like* therapy because all I ever do is ask very peculiar questions, questions that I do not preface with any explanation or justification. For some, it looks like these questions arise randomly and spontaneously, without any apparent connection to the pattern(s) of the conversation prior to the question, while for those more familiar with my way of doing therapy, these questions seem clearly chosen and precisely timed in order to help me and my clients figure out what to do.

It has always seemed to me that rigorous descriptions of what works, including decision-making criteria for figuring out what to do in specific clinical situations, are sufficient. But the question "How does it work?" always seems to arise. My position has been that one cannot know how it works, one can only know that it does work. Answers to the question "How does it work?" always involve speculation.

> **speculation, 1**: to meditate; to contemplate; to consider a subject by turning it in the mind and viewing it in its different aspects and relations. **2**: to think about or theorize on any subject; to reason from assumed premises; to conjecture.

And to speculate, to conjecture, is a matter of storytelling; it is fiction. Therefore, until quite recently, my response to the question "How does it work?" has been "Make up your own explanation: It is as good or better than mine." In this I followed Wittgenstein: "Our mistake is to look for an explanation where we ought to look at what happens" (1968, #654).

In workshops and training sessions, I have recently begun to offer some new forms of description, new metaphors – not causal speculations, but attempts to clarify through borrowed metaphors that I thought might not obscure what happens. I was afraid these would be too simplistic for the trainees and workshop participants; however, I have been surprised at how readily these have been accepted. Even more recently, I have begun to offer some abstract, conceptual metaphors based on an intellectual framework more encompassing than is common in the family therapy or brief therapy discourse. Again, I have been surprised by how well these sometimes very general, abstract ideas seem to be accepted.

To my surprise or even wonder, rather than serving to digress the workshop conversation away from the pragmatics of solution-focused brief therapy, ideas from philosophy of language seemed to open doors for some people and help them figure out what works or what might work. Sometimes, in fact, these metaphors seemed to help some people *see* what happens in the various clinical situations I use as illustrations.

* * *

This book will focus on critical readings that, to me, seem to be useful in thinking about what it is that is going on in the clinical situation and in *seeing* what happens in therapy. This book will, therefore, deal with concepts and the relationships between concepts that seem to lie at the center of describing therapy, thinking about therapy, and in particular, thinking about doing therapy. While some of the thinking will recast concepts I have previously dealt with, I will also borrow heavily from various authors in various fields of endeavor whose thinking seems to validate and amplify my long secret way of thinking about things. Rather than borrowing a whole frame-work, I have borrowed selectively and purposefully – a concept from here, one from there, and another from yet somewhere else. The framework is mine and, although it is related to other frameworks, I am the one responsible for whether it is coherent or incoherent. Obviously, some readers will agree with me in thinking that it is coherent, while others will think it borders on nonsense. My hope for both groups of readers is that it does not distract them from doing therapy in a useful and effective fashion.

* * *

Although it deals more with thinking about therapy and thinking about doing therapy, this work, like my previous work, is directly connected to observing what happens in therapy.

At times I have been alone observing what Insoo Kim Berg and her clients did in therapy; at other times I have been joined by various colleagues. I have, both alone and with colleagues, watched videotapes of what my clients and I did in therapy sessions and I have watched what my colleagues and their clients did in therapy. For me and my colleagues it is always interesting to watch what Insoo and her clients do in therapy because we base our clinical work on trying to do with our clients what she does with hers.

This book is a series of essays, narratives, and/or critical readings that forms part of a discourse about an endeavor known by the general labels "therapy," "family therapy," and more particularly, "brief therapy." Unlike my previous books and most of my professional writing, there will be little about actually *doing* therapy here. Rather, the focus here will be on *describing* therapy, *thinking* about therapy and thinking about *doing* therapy.

This book will also have little to say about the pragmatics of doing therapy. It is not a replacement for *Clues: Investigating Solutions in Brief Therapy* (de Shazer, 1988), just as *Clues* was not a replacement for *Keys to Solution in Brief Therapy* (de Shazer, 1985). Each book is, as it were, a whole, complete world, a perspective from a particular point of view. *Keys* might be seen as written from a "practice" point of view, *Clues* from a research, or better a "searching" or investigative point of view, and this book from a "theorizing" or critical point of view. Hence the analysis is different, although what it is that is being analyzed remains the same: *Doing brief therapy.*

* * *

It is important to recognize that this is not an underlying or overarching theory that I am developing in this book. It is just another narrative, another way of describing what brief therapists and clients *do* when they are doing brief therapy and, perhaps more broadly, what therapists and clients in general do when they are doing therapy. This theoretical analysis or critical reading is on the same level as practice and research. Theory, research/search, and practice all guide, influence, and change each other. For example, a change in practice (if it is a difference that seems to make a difference) will suggest a new area for disciplined observation (or search) which, in turn, will send the theorist to the library looking for a frame or frames to help him describe things in a clear and useful manner.

What is developed in this book is certainly not a Theory with a capital T; rather, the analysis leads away from such a grand design, emphasizing instead the variability of the clinical situation and the people involved (both clients and therapists), the variability of events, and the variability of problems and solutions.

There is no stability of point of view from within a given perspective. For example, during the process of disciplined observation, the points of view might include (but are not limited to): (a) the therapist in front of the mirror, (b) the team behind the mirror, (c) the engineer developing an expert system, and (d) the theorist developing maps and flow charts. Similarly, when developing a theoretical perspective or a critical reading, various points of view might be useful. At times these points of view overlap; at times they might be confusing, even contradictory. This is not problematic but inevitable: Where you stand determines what you see and what you do not see; it determines also the angle you see it from; a change in where you stand changes everything.

Although Ludwig Wittgenstein, Jacques Derrida, Paul de Man, Ernst von Glasersfeld, Paul Watzlawick, Milton Erickson, etc., see things from different points of view, both the similarities and the differences among their viewpoints can be informative and useful to a clear description and analysis.

Putting Difference to Work

Part One

1

AN ATTEMPT TO READ
"FAMILY THERAPY"

The classifications made by philosophers and psychologists are like those that someone would give who tried to classify clouds by their shapes.

— Wittgenstein, 1975a, #154

Looking at the vast array of books that have come out in the past 30 years dealing with "family therapy," the various professional journals, *Family Process, Journal of Marital and Family Therapy, The American Journal of Family Therapy, Perheterapia, Contemporary Family Therapy, Familiendynamik, Zeitschrift für systemische Therapie, Journal of Strategic and Systemic Therapies, Systeme, The Australian and New Zealand Journal of Family Therapy, Fokus På Familien, Family Therapy Case Studies*, etc., etc., and attending conferences organized by the American Family Therapy Association, the *Family Therapy Networker*, and the American Association for Marriage and Family Therapy (and, if one follows the network of presenters, the conferences organized by the Erickson Foundation), etc., can leave one wondering about what the term "family therapy" might mean. What is it that is left over that is somehow "the same" once all that is idiosyncratic to the various schools ("structural family therapy," "behavioral family therapy," etc.) is eliminated? What is it that remains that is even somehow "similar" enough for all of them to be called "family therapy?"

Even watching various "family therapists" at work with

their clients (sometimes a family group, sometimes a couple, sometimes an individual, sometimes a group of families) leaves the observer wondering what is it that these therapists mean when they all say that they are doing "family therapy." Clearly, the authors, readers, presenters, and participants behave as if there is something – certainly not methods or techniques, but perhaps a concept called "family therapy" – that unites them – an observation that is further promoted by the existence of professional organizations. And yet, what is it? The differences between and among "family therapists" are quite clear in comparison to the similarities. Obviously, there is a discourse called "family therapy" (a practice that forms the "object" of which it speaks); there must also be a field called "family therapy" since there are degrees and licenses. But what are the boundaries between "family therapy" and "non-family-therapy"? Where does one draw the distinction? What is framed by the frame "family therapy"? What is "inside" this frame? What is "outside" this frame? What does "family therapy" mean?

* * *

To start with, it might be interesting to note that the dictionary defines therapy in this way:

> **therapy**, that part of medical science which relates to the treatment and cure of diseases; concerned in discovering and applying remedies for diseases. from the Greek *therapeuein*, to nurse, serve, or cure;

it defines "science" as

> systematized knowledge derived from observation, study, and experimentation carried on in order to determine the nature or principles of what is being studied;

and "disease" as

> a particular destructive process in the body, with a specific cause and characteristic symptoms.

Generally, the term therapy as used in this book is a nickname or shortened form of the terms (a) family therapy, (b) brief therapy, and/or (c) psychotherapy.

> **psychotherapy,** the application of various forms of mental
> treatment to nervous and mental disorders.

A further definition of "psycho-" is

> meaning mind or mental processes. from the Greek *psy-
> che*, soul;

and mental

> **mental,** 1: of or for the mind or intellect; 2: done by or
> carried on in, the mind; 3: diseased in mind; mentally ill.
> from the latin *mentalis*, of or pertaining to the mind *syn*.
> psychological, intellectual, psychical, metaphysical.

Probably the term "family therapy" was first used without
much thought, used simply to distinguish a new way of doing
therapy different from the dominant way of doing therapy that
involved just an individual. For instance, 30 years ago, "family
therapy" would mean that an individual with a diagnosis of
schizophrenia was being seen with the other members of the
family rather than alone.

> **diagnosis,** the act or process of deciding the nature of a
> diseased condition by examination. from the Greek *dia*,
> between and *gignoskein*, to know.

In family therapy, the disease of the individual was recast as a
disease of the family or the family system. Thirty years later it
might be difficult to see how radical and revolutionary this
move from individual to family, this resituating of the "disease"
from individual to family, "from psyche to system"[1] was.

---

[1] I am going to deliberately leave the term "system" undefined until Chapter 2
except to say that, in family therapy, it has something to do with the relationship between the members of a system.

Thus, one way to read the term "family therapy" might be to see it as a remedy for some disease of the family, particularly some disease involving the family's mind or mental processes. Today, not many family therapists are going to be comfortable with such a reading, definition, or understanding of the term family therapy, although some family therapists think in terms of "undifferentiated family ego mass" (Bowen, 1966) and other labels carried over from psychodynamic tradition (Titchener, 1967).

The move from psyche to system suggests another, different reading: Family therapy is a remedy for some disease of the family, particularly some disease involving the family's system, whatever "system" means here (a replacement for the term psyche?). But, what kind of disease is involved here? A mental disease, a disease of the mind, or a disease of the soul? What kind of diagnosis is involved? Can we read the term "system" to stand for the mind of the family or the soul of the family as if the family was some sort of supra-individual? If we redesign the word "disease" into the term "dis-ease"

dis-ease, an obsolete form meaning uneasiness or distress,

then more family therapists will be at least somewhat comfortable with the reading.

Or perhaps family therapy was intended simply to draw a distinction between this new therapy and the dominant Freudian (or psychodynamic) therapy, which would suggest that it is a type of therapy based on a different set of principles.

Book after book, and article after article written by family therapists leave the reader no better off, since most authors assume that their definition of family therapy is the same as that of their readers. Ackerman (1966) is an exception:

Family psychotherapy is defined as a special method of treatment of emotional disorders, based on dynamically oriented interviews with the whole family. It is the therapy of a natural living unit, embracing all these persons who share the identity of family and whose behavior is influenced by a circular inter-change of emotion. . . . The family is viewed as a behavioral sys-tem with emergent properties different from a mere summation of the characteristics of its members. The behavior of any one member may be interpreted in four ways: as a symptom of the psychopathology of the family unit; as a stabilizer of the family; as healer of family disorder, and as the epitome of growth po-tential of the group. Treatment focuses on the relations be-tween the psychosocial functioning of the family group and the emotional functioning of its members. (Ackerman, 1966, p. 406)

Beels and Ferber (1973) are another exception. They define family therapy by comparing it to various types of individual therapy which the see as having four common elements:

(a) There are two people in confidential interaction;
(b) the mode of interaction is usually verbal;
(c) the interaction is relatively prolonged; and
(d) the relationship has for its definite and agreed-upon purpose changes in the behavior of one of the participants [presum-ably the client!].

For Beels and Ferber, family therapy differs in these ways:

(a) There are *more* than two people, and the interaction between them is to that important extent *not* confidential . . . the change of technique in the jump from a dyadic to triadic (or more) interaction is a discontinuous one.
(b) Nonverbal interaction assumes a primary importance along with the verbal; manipulation of membership, gestures, seat-ing arrangement and posture, by any and all participants, is significant.
(c) It is often shorter than individual therapy, but this is enor-mously variable.
(d) The relationship has for its definite and agreed-upon purpose changes in the family *system* of interaction, not changes in the behavior of individuals. *Individual change occurs as a by-product of system change.* (Beels & Ferber, 1973, p. 172) [emphasis added; see below]

Stierlin (1977) also noted some of the differences between psychoanalysis and family therapy:

> Family theory implies a system rather than an individual (or at best a dyadic) approach, that observable transactions often have primacy over inferable intrapsychic processes, and that therapeutic activism may be more effective than a passive furtherance of insight. Also, we must accept the fact that family theorists and therapists needed to create a new language that befitted their subject and, in some respects, was scientifically more up to date than that of psychoanalysis. To a large extent, this was the language of modern cybernetics. (p. 13)

This gets us further in the attempt to read family therapy. We now know that both individual and family therapy involve talking (verbal interaction), but family therapy seems to involve more than two people sitting and talking. Family therapy calls on the therapist to be more active in some way(s). We also know that there is some time distinction, individual therapy being "prolonged" and family therapy being "shorter." (It is not clear whether the time distinction drawn by Beels and Ferber refers to the length of the sessions, the number of sessions, and/or the length of the whole treatment process.)

"*Individual change occurs as a by-product of system change*" (Beels & Ferber, 1973, p. 172). Here Beels and Ferber describe a very radical move, a gambit central to the development of family therapy, a move which accords individual change a secondary status as a by-product to systemic change. Through this inversion, a type of change occurs which Foucault (1972) calls a "redistribution" (a change brought about by a reversal in hierarchical order); that which was primary, the individual, has become secondary and that which was secondary, the family, has become primary. This shift, a difference that makes a difference, is so radical that it is difficult to contain or even include it within the traditional "mental health" discourse. Social, organizational, interactional, and familial principles, rather than psychodynamic ones, are involved in the shift from psyche to system.

But how can the treatment of a "mental disorder," which is

seen as a problem of the individual's psyche, be based on principles that are social or interactional or familial? How is this "outside," this social context, connected with the inside? What is the relationship of individual to system, system to individual?

*   *   *

Jackson and Weakland (1961) describe family therapy as "treating the identified patient and other members of his family together as a functioning natural group" (p. 30). Paul (1967) describes marital therapy as a variant of family therapy and sees it as "a psychotherapeutic setting designed to treat both the marital partners and the transactional interface between them, i.e., the marriage" (p. 186), and Zuk (1967) describes family therapy as "the technique that explores and attempts to shift the balance of pathogenic relating among family members so that new forms of relating become possible" (p. 72).

A variety of family therapy was developed at the Mental Research Institute that was based more on an anthropological or sociological view than on a psychiatric view. As part of a larger study on communication, they attempted to develop a theoretical framework that described the minimal conditions under which schizophrenic communication might seem both reasonable and natural (Bateson, Jackson, Haley, & Weakland, 1956). For this purpose, and being oriented toward anthropology, they began to observe "schizophrenics" interacting with their families, i.e., their natural group. They described the "schizophrenic's" communication as a reasonable response to a communication pattern they labeled "double binds" and developed a model of therapy based on a similar therapeutic pattern they called a "counter double bind" which subsequently was extended beyond the treatment of "schizophrenics in their families" to other problems brought to therapists and thus to human communication in general (Watzlawick et al., 1967). From this perspective, Haley (1967a) develops what Foucault (1972) calls a "mutation," a type of change that displaces the boundaries around the concept of family therapy and takes the inversion mentioned by Beels and Ferber radically further. He writes that "the various methods of family therapy that have appeared would seem to have one factor in common: a focus on the problem of coalition both within the family and between therapist and family members" (1967a, p. 25). He continues . . .

> certain factions of a family might be more accessible to change than others. In schizophrenia, for example, the parents and schizophrenic child might be the triangle most resistant to change so that treatment of another section of the family could produce better results. Yet to suggest this possibility indicates how rapid a change has been taking place in psychiatry. Not many years ago, it was thought a waste of time to attempt psychotherapy with a schizophrenic. More recently, it has seemed pointless to treat *only* the schizophrenic, because of his involvement with his parents (and the hospital staff), who should also enter treatment. Now it is conceivable that the schizophrenic could be treated without ever entering therapy since a change in him is assumed to be brought about if another part of the extended family in which he lives is changed. (p. 26)

In fact, in the report of a much ignored family therapy research project (see Langsley, Pittman, Machotka, & Flomenhaft, 1968), Pittman, Langsley, Flomenhaft, DeYoung, Machotka, and Kaplan (1971) describe doing family therapy with

> anyone [who was] involved . . . and then negotiations continued with whatever combination of people might most naturally negotiate the conflictual issues. Ordinarily, therapy narrowed down to the two or three people most directly involved in the crisis and included the decision-making hierarchy of the family. Even the identified patient might be excluded early in treatment. Family therapy might involve, all along, only one family member, perhaps not the identified patient. (p. 262)

Clearly, "family therapy is not simply therapy with families, but rather a form of therapy in which the identified patients are treated in conjunction with their relevant social context, which may consist of the immediate family but can also include friends and members of the wider family" (Lange & van der Hart, 1983, p. 18).

Now, what in the world could family therapy mean? A treatment method designed to treat a mental illness (e.g., schizophrenia) for a shorter rather than prolonged time by sitting and talking with some members of the patient's (the schizophrenic's) family, excluding the (so-called) patient but perhaps including some friends of the patient or family? How can we possibly read the term family therapy?

Although these citations are mainly quite early in the evolution and development of family therapy, the situation today is little better, even among family therapy researchers where definitional rigor is required.

For instance, Stanton (1988) defines family therapy, or perhaps more appropriately, systems therapy, as

> an approach in which a therapist (or a team of therapists), working with varying combinations and configurations of people, devises and introduces interventions designed to alter the interaction (process, workings) of the interpersonal system and context within which one or more psychiatric/behavioral/human problems are embedded, and thereby also alters the functioning of the individuals within that system, with the goal of alleviating or eliminating the problems. (p. 9)

> > **intervention:** 1: a state of coming or being between. 2: interposition, mediation; any interference in the affairs of others.

Gurman's (1988) description of family therapy is:

> 1. At the broadest level, family therapy may be defined by *the conceptual "map"* in the mind of the therapist, such that if therapists regularly and systematically consider the family context, then they are doing family therapy irrespective of who is in the consultation room or how many people are present. . . . A related but more midrange definition would define family therapy by *the therapist's intent for the outcome.*

That is, by whom do they aim to influence – symptomatic or distressed persons only, the family as a whole,[2] or all individuals, including nonfamily members, who are clinically relevant?

2. The most restrictive definition focuses only on the *persons who are present* in treatment sessions. By this criterion, face-to-face treatment of an individual would not be included in the definition of "family therapy," regardless of the therapist's conceptual map or outcome intent. Family therapy requires the presence and treatment of two or more related individuals. (p. 125)

Epstein (1988) sees family therapy as

a therapeutic approach to working with the family unit as a system for the purpose of aiding the family members to achieve solutions to problems that interfere with their satisfactory functioning as individuals and as a family unit. (p. 120)

Neither Hoffman in her book *Foundations of Family Therapy* (1981) nor Simon, Stierlin, and Wynne (1985) in their book *The Language of Family Therapy: A Systemic Vocabulary and Sourcebook* attempt to define "family therapy," although Simon et al. do describe the various types or schools of family therapy. For instance:

A structurally oriented therapist sees the first task as the assessment of dysfunctional structures in the family, such as blurring of boundaries, confusion in the family hierarchy, and the existence of rigid, pathological coalitions. Further, it is generally believed to be essential that the therapist "join" the family, which means to attune oneself to the manner in which the family thinks, speaks, and feels. The therapist often imitates the family's style (in mimesis) and takes up the family's images, expectations, and metaphors. The therapist may "track" the family interaction by allowing, or even encouraging family patterns to unfold naturally before intervening overtly.

---

[2]Yet, as my colleague Ron Kral points out, family therapy has no Diagnostic and Statistical Manual by which to define either "illness" or "health" in families.

The therapist then uses a variety of techniques to restructure diffuse or rigid boundaries of the family as a whole and its subsystems, thereby enabling the development of new and more effective problem-solving strategies and correcting patterns of enmeshment and disengagement. . . . Whenever possible, the therapist supports the leadership of the parents and seeks to break up dysfunctional, cross-generational structures in which the children take on aspects of parental roles. (Simon, Stierlin, & Wynne, 1985, p. 339–340)

Thus, for structural family therapists the dis-ease or dysfunction involves the structural and/or hierarchical misalignment of family relationships. It is this structure, known through a structural diagnosis, that is the patient or client being treated for a dis-ease resulting from some specific cause with characteristic symptoms, specifically the so-called "psychosomatic family," and more generally, "enmeshed and disengaged families." It is this abstract structure of family relationship, *not* the family members as a group and *not* the individual family members, that is the focus of family therapy in general and structural family therapy in particular.

At times it can be difficult for a family therapist to recognize that the therapy he is watching (or reading about) is *really* family therapy. For instance, you might hear Weakland (1982) talking about "'Family Therapy' with Individuals" and you might read de Shazer and Berg (1984) describing doing marital therapy with just one of the partners. So, perhaps we need to settle for a definition once offered a workshop participant: Family therapy is what family therapists do when they say they are doing family therapy.

Clearly, these citations are not exhaustive or comprehensive and they were not selected randomly. The sample was selected intentionally to give you, the reader, some idea of the difficulties therapists, readers, and authors have defining concepts. Many other citations from various other authors writing about family therapy could have been selected and would have demonstrated the same difficulty in reading the term family therapy. Perhaps surprisingly, what is included under the label family therapy is no more clear than what is excluded.

* * *

Perhaps the only way to know what family therapy is is to watch family therapists at work. Then it is plain to see that two or more people (at least one person called a family therapist and at least one person called a client or patient) are sitting and talking (for a shorter rather than a more prolonged time). What they talk about and how they talk about it differs widely, but it is usually clear that they are talking about something problematic for the client, and frequently what they talk about is clearly focused on the interactional aspects of someone's dis-ease (who may or may not be present), about which the client is concerned.

But, perhaps only the fact that two or more people are sitting and talking together would be obvious to a naive observer. Perhaps this experience of naively watching family therapy would be similar to looking through a microscope for the first time and seeing only bubbles, hairs, and worms instead of the microorganisms that a trained observer sees.

Although this more or less unified and minimal definition seems to get at the minimal criteria for reading the term family therapy, nonetheless one would be hard pressed to use the definition to exclude any particular therapy session of any kind. The difficulty with "family therapy" as a concept is that it is hard to distinguish "family therapy" from "non-family-therapy" and thus the concept loses the difference that makes a difference.

The above attempt to read the concept "family therapy" would only have been successful if you, the reader, were to be able to figure out what is common to all the examples and, therefore, to apply the concept "family therapy" to a next instance, a new example and be able to say that it is either "inside" or "outside" the concept's definition. But failing to be able to do this does not necessarily make the concept defective: It still has some sort of unity that we can perhaps show[3]. This

---

[3]For instance, we can point to the professional organizations as showing the unity of the concept "family therapy."

situation has at least one major, desirable aspect: It prevents some school of family therapy from claiming to be the bearer of "true" family therapy.

FAMILY[4] RESEMBLANCE CONCEPTS

The philosopher Ludwig Wittgenstein analyzes ill-defined or fuzzy concepts, such as the concept of family therapy, and designates them "family resemblance concepts": i.e., concepts with no unified definition, concepts involving some similarities that are readily apparent and others that require extended observations and thought. This similarity involves "a complicated network of similarities overlapping and criss-crossing: sometimes overall similarities, sometimes similarities of details" (Wittgenstein, 1968, #66). Indeed, comparison of many different examples of family therapy is perhaps the only way to explain what is meant by the concept family therapy. Interestingly, the multiplicity of similarities and differences in family resemblance concepts leads us off in many directions, emphasizing the need for looking at context and the ways the concept is used to help us avoid nonsense and rubbish.

Wittgenstein's classic example of a family resemblance concept is the concept of "game." We all think we know what a game is, but it turns out that a unified definition is impossible. For instance, we might start with basketball as an example of a game. There are ten players, five on each side; there is a spherical ball that is either passed from one player to another or bounced on the floor until it is shot at a basket. Some shots count for three points, some for two, some for one, etc. Now, let's take another activity called a game, poker. A similar description would be very different, and yet we intuitively know that basketball and poker are both games. Certainly, both are similarly competitive: One team or one player wins while others lose. Solitaire is also a game, somewhat similar to poker and

---

[4]This use of the word "family" as part of the idea of "family resemblance" has nothing whatsoever to do with families per se or with family therapy. This word in the name of the concept is just meant to get at the idea that the resemblance between any defining members of a concept is sort of like the resemblances found between various members of the same family.

yet somehow very different. And then there are borderline cases: Is a team practicing basketball involved in a game? How about the individual in a driveway? Or the coach's chalkboard diagrams?

* * *

Although the concepts deal with throughout this book are sometimes treated as largely separate and independent concepts, each of them is also related to the others. As part of reading the book, readers and the author will, at times, link them together to produce the patterns of the cultural activity known as reading a book. Perhaps you, the reader, will make different links than I do. Reading is, after all, a creative activity.

The concepts dealt with under the general heading of family therapy, like the concept family therapy itself, are not as simple as they seem at first glance. Most of the concepts have no collective definition like those found in a dictionary. The concepts that will be dealt with in this book are all family resemblance concepts. No unified definition of them is possible because all of the examples of each concept, like the various definitions of family therapy, involve aspects that are absent from other examples also classified under the same conceptual label.

It is equally clear that each and every example of a concept is in some ways similar to others categorized with it. It might not be going too far to say that one definition of family therapy is similar to another in the same way that a musical variation is similar to its theme: But, as is true sometimes in the jazz world, the theme is unstated.

2

THE CONCEPT OF SYSTEM

In the family therapy discourse, the term "system" appears perhaps more frequently than any other word. This is not accidental since it is a commonly held assumption among family therapists that "system theory" or "systems theory" or "general systems theory" is what links the models or schools of family therapy together. "Systems theory" is seen by many as the essence of family therapy.

> General systems theory influenced family therapy in two ways. It provided a conceptual framework which some people felt could be used to describe or even explain family phenomena. The fact that it is so abstract, however, created great confusion. . . . (Lange & van der Hart, 1983, p. 6)

According to the dictionary:

> system, 1: a set or arrangement of things so related or connected as to form a unity or organic whole. 2: the world or universe. 3: the body considered as a functioning organism. 4: a set of facts, principles, rules, etc., classified or arranged in a regular, orderly form so as to show a logical plan linking the various parts.

Following this, we need to narrow the scope, bringing the term "system" into therapeutic discourse with a relatively early definition:

> system . . . a set of objects together with relationships be-
> tween the objects and between their attributes. (Hall &
> Fagan, 1956, p. 18)

But this is far too nonspecific even for the highly abstract general systems theory and still leaves us wondering, "What kind of system is being talked about when family therapists and brief therapists use the term?"

As Lynn Hoffman (1971) put it, "The question of what is a system is a vexing one." In her view, "The most common defini-tion seems to be: any entity the parts of which covary interde-pendently with one another, and which maintains equilibrium in an error-activated way" (p. 286).

HOW CAN WE READ "SYSTEM" WITHIN
THE FRAME OF FAMILY THERAPY?

Having postponed defining the omnipresent, ubiquitous term "system" as a concept central to family therapy until this point, we could do worse than a definition provided for this context (the family therapy discourse) by Simon et al. (1985):

> The most general definition of system [Greek *systema*, a com-
> posite thing] is the ordered composition of (material or mental)
> elements into a unified whole. . . . General systems theory, like
> cybernetics, concerns itself with the functions and structural
> rules valid for all systems, irrespective of their material consti-
> tution. The premises of systems theory are based on the insight
> that a system as a whole is qualitatively different, and "be-
> haves" differently, from the sum of the system's individual ele-
> ments. (Simon et al., 1985, p. 353)

This "cybernetics" Simon et al. (1985) use as a comparison to the term "system"

> is based on the supposition that the functions of control, regula-
> tion, information exchange, and information processing follow
> the same principles regardless of whether they are applied to
> machines, organisms, or social structures. (p. 82)

Clearly, Simon et al.'s definition is one that makes sense within the context of how the term system was used in Chapter 1. But what kind of system are family therapists talking about?

> The family-rules theory fits the initial definition of a system as "stable with respect to certain of its variables if these variables tend to remain within defined limits," and in fact this suggests a more formal consideration of *the family as a system*.
>
> Such a model for family interaction was proposed by Jackson when he introduced the concept of family homeostasis. Observing that the families of psychiatric patients often demonstrated drastic repercussions (depression, psychosomatic attacks, and the like) when the patient improved, he postulated that these behaviors and perhaps therefore the patient's illness as well were "homeostatic mechanisms," operating to bring the disturbed system back into its delicate balance. This brief statement is the core of a communication approach to the family. (Watzlawick et al., 1967, p. 134) [Emphasis added]

That is, in the family therapy discourse, the family can be seen as if it were a system or, better, the family can be described with many of the same tools used to describe any system. "The family can be regarded as a system in many respects: a system of communication, a power system, an affective system" (Lange & van der Hart, 1983, p. 7). The family can also be described as a social system, a behavioral system, an interactional system, a cultural system, a games system, a biological system, an emotional system, a relationship system, etc. In any case, "system" is an abstraction involving the perception that the whole is different from the sum of the system's parts and that systems, regardless of what kind of parts or elements are involved, can be seen to follow some general rules. "The family *is* a system in that a change in one part of the system is followed by compensatory change in other parts of the system" (Bowen, 1966, p. 152).

And there are other definitions from social science and philosophy, for instance this one from Anthony Wilden (1980):

A system is distinguished from its parts by its organization.
. . . The behavior of the whole is more complex than the "sum" of
the "behavior" of its parts. However, since the organization of
the whole imposes *constraints* on the "behavior" of the parts, we
must also recognize that the semiotic freedom of each subsystem in itself is greater than its semiotic freedom as a part of the
whole, and may in effect by greater than that of the whole. (p.
202–203)[1]

For Wilden, then, an individual word or a behavior, when it
stands alone, has more freedom of meaning than it does when
it is part of a conversation or interaction. The meaning of a
word or a behavior is constrained or limited by the particular
system since its meaning is the subject of negotiation.

Although both Simon et al. (1985) and Wilden (1980) talk
about "behavior," for the former a system involves something
mental or material, while for the latter a system involves signs
and meanings; this seems related to the definition of Watzlawick, Beavin, and Jackson (1967) "interactional systems shall
be two or more communicants in the process of, or at the level
of, defining the nature of their relationship" (p. 121), where
communication is the behavior talked about.

As we will continue to see, these widely differing definitions
play havoc, creating muddle after muddle, within the field of
family therapy (and related fields).

Before we go any further, systems, in general, are seen to
have the following attributes or properties.

---

[1]**semiotic, 1:** of signs or sign language. **2:** in medicine, (a) of symp-
        toms; (b) symptomatic.
The dictionary definition might lead to a misreading based on structuralist
thinking, the assumption that signs are symptoms of some deeper meaning,
i.e., Chomsky's idea (1968) that signs are but surface manifestations of a deep
structure where meaning lies. Semiotics is not to be confused with syntax,
which concerns the relationship between words and sentence structure, or
semantics, which concerns the relationship between the sign and what it signi-
fies. In this particular discourse, semiotics might better be defined as an area
of study that investigates the pragmatic relationship among: (a) sign, (b) sign-
giver, and (c) sign-receiver. (See Chapters 3 through 5.)

1. *Wholeness*: A change in one part of a system necessarily affects the whole system.
2. *Nonsummativity*: The whole is different from the sum of its parts.
3. *Equifinality, multifinality: Equifinality* means that the final state may be reached from different initial states and/or by different paths; *multifinality* means that similar initial conditions, and/or routing by different paths, may lead to dissimilar end-states.
4. *Circular causality, nonlinearity*: "The relationship of the progression of causes is such that the initial cause is also affected by the progression itself" (Simon et al., p. 212) which is contrasted with linearity in which "feedback processes are not involved . . . the cause-effect sequence does not lead back to the starting point" (Simon et al., 1985, p. 212).

A SYSTEMIC MUDDLE

According to Auerswald (1987), five different "paradigms" (Auerswald does not define his use of this term but his use of the term "paradigm" seems close to the Kuhnian sense of the term)[2] have developed in "family therapy" each of which is based on a different definition of family system:

1. A *psychodynamic* paradigm in which a family is defined as a group made up of the interlocking psychodynamics of its members . . . ;
2. a *family system* paradigm, which defines a family as a system that operates independently, and from which individual psychodynamics, including those that create symptoms, emerge;
3. a *general systems* paradigm in which a family is defined as a system that shares isomorphic characteristics with all systems . . . ;
4. a *cybernetic systems* paradigm, which defines a system, in-

---

[2]*Paradigm*, "what the members of a scientific community share, and, conversely, a scientific community consists of men who share a paradigm." (Kuhn, 1970, p. 176)

cluding a family system, in terms of circular information flow and regulatory mechanisms; and

5. an *ecological systems* (*ecosystemic*) paradigm, which defines a family as a coevolutionary ecosystem located in evolutionary timespace. (p. 321–322)

A simple substitution equation follows from both Chapter 1 and the systemic views looked at so far:

$$\text{individual} = \text{family}$$
$$\text{psyche} = \text{system.}$$

Simply, the family has been substituted for the individual and the system has been substituted for the psyche. That is, in "family therapy sessions, 'the patient' is the family, not any individual" (Wynne, 1971, p. 100).

Gerald Erickson's critique (1988)[3] points to one result of the difficulties involved with this substitution:

The traps laid by systemic family analysis are springing up everywhere and they permit no easy escape. The currently *hegemonic circular-systemic paradigm*, marked as it is by three powerful and negative ideals of our time—anti-humanism, anti-subjectivism, and anti-historicism—has *inevitably* led to forms of analysis whereby families are taken as closed systems, where relations among members are given primacy, a division of the relations into manifest/latent functions taken as a given, and wherein only the therapist is privileged to interpret latent function. None of the major human problems of our era can be adequately addressed by, or treated within, *a systemic paradigm*, whether child abuse, the situations of formerly hospitalized individuals, gender inequality, problems of spousal violence, or social inequality. *Such problems either cannot be perceived within a systemic view . . . or, if attention is called to them, must* necessarily *disappear into a set of interlocking and circular relations, the sum of which are* [sic] *said to serve a purpose of coherence and fit, of being homeostatic and helpful, of being required*

[3]Ignoring for now the various other muddles involved in Erickson's paper, i.e., the confusion of map, interpretation, and territory (see de Shazer, 1989).

by the family, of being wanted and desired. (p. 225–6) [Emphasis added]

Erickson suggests, through his use of the term *a systemic paradigm*, that his critique applies universally, to any and all systemic paradigms. At the very least, however, his critique leaves open the question of boundaries: What system is he talking about? First Erickson talks about the "family system," then apparently switches to some larger social systems. In either case, he wants us to believe that "coherence, fit, homeostasis" (concepts that are part of one model, perhaps more than one model, but not all, or perhaps, one paradigm but not all) are concepts that are used by all systemic thinkers, and therefore, that all systemic paradigms are inadequate in the same way. Vincent Fish (1990) joins Erickson is this muddle, when he critiques the inadequacies of "*the systemic paradigm*" (pp. 21–24) – as if there were only one – and *the* systemic paradigm, according to Fish, is limited to the views developed from the work of Gregory Bateson.

At least in part, this sort of muddle is the result of the reversal of the hierarchy, the simple substitution of terms that still maintains the therapist as an independent observer of what he is observing, the subject-object split long discarded by twentieth-century science and philosophy (see Wechsler, 1978) and given lip-service, as we shall see, by many family therapists.

Hall and Fagan (1956), pioneers of general systems theory, ask a pertinent question in this regard: When does an object belong to a system and when does an object belong to the system's environment?

If an object reacts with a system in the way described above [see the attributes of systems above] should it not be considered part of the system? The answer is by no means definite. In a sense, a system together with its environment makes up the universe of all things of interest within a given context. Subdivision of this universe into two sets, system and environment, can be done in many ways which are in fact quite arbitrary.... (p. 20)

Family therapy has, on the whole, failed to see that family therapy can itself be seen or described as a system and has been blind about the ramifications of a systemic view of therapy – that systemic attributes and properties apply to the description of the therapeutic system as such. That is, what is going on in therapy can be described and analyzed using systems theory. The therapist interacts with the client, and this interaction can be seen as connected with the client in such a way that the therapist cannot be split off and assigned to a detached, independent observer's position. In the therapy situation, the client(s) and the therapist are the "communicants in the process of, or at the level of, defining the nature of their relationship" (Watzlawick et al. 1967, p. 121). As we saw in the above examples (Erickson's critique and the critique by Fish), and as we will see again in Chapter 3, splitting a whole system into parts leads to imaginary oppositions and pathological communication (Wilden, 1980). The systemic revolution is not systemic enough; it has not gone far enough.

Thus, when talking about "family *therapy*," not about families-in-therapy, it is necessary to add a sixth paradigm (here using "paradigm" as Auerswald uses the term), the *therapy situation as a system* (de Shazer, 1982a, 1982b), which defines the system under consideration as involving the construction of a purposeful system composed of (a) the therapist subsystem, (b) the client subsystem, (c) the problem to be solved and/ or the solution to be developed, and (d) the interactions and interrelationships between and among the first three (de Shazer, 1985, 1988).

The usefulness of this distinction between (a) seeing family therapy as concerned with the *family system* (all of Auerswald's five "paradigms") and (b) seeing therapy as concerned with the *therapy situation as a system* will be explored in subsequent chapters. Each perspective leads to drawing a methodological boundary around a different area of concern or interest, with profound repercussions, consequences, and ramifications for how therapists view their job and situation.

* * *

Ever since Freud's efforts to develop a scientific psychology, therapeutic discourse has attempted to be scientific, to use the metaphors of science, and therefore, to use positivistic assumptions and emulate scientific methods of research. Certainly, this is one approach to disciplining observations, and therefore, being able to describe, with some rigor, what it is that is going on. But there is no reason to privilege the positivistic point of view or the positivistic paradigm.

Metaphors borrowed from physical science as explanations or explanatory metaphors in family therapy (with a barrier between the participants) move the family therapy discourse away from language, away from observing what clients and therapists do in therapy. Using this sort of metaphor, what lies behind and beneath is seen as more basic than what can actually be observed to happen in therapy. The explanatory metaphor takes precedence over the language, hiding or at least obscuring the conversation, which is the most readily discernible feature of all therapy.

Of course, this situation is not unique to contemporary family therapy. Traditionally, therapists have devoted a large part of their intellectual project to dealing with various kinds of analysis, searching for the etiology of client's problems in hopes that understanding this etiology would lead to resolving the client's problem. While in Freud's day the problem was seen to "reside" in the psyche (interior to the person and behind the words), in family therapy the problem was seen to reside in the system (exterior to the person but, nonetheless, behind the words). In both cases, the explanatory metaphors, psyche and system, lost their status as metaphor and became real enough to be seen as more central to therapy than the words involved in the conversation.

It is, of course, altogether too easy to reify concepts and explanatory metaphors. The little phrase "as if" is most easily ignored and even lost by accident or deliberately discarded. It is but a simple step from "The family can be seen as if it were a system" to "The family is a system," from saying "The rules of general system theory help us make sense of our observations of families" to saying that "The family does what it does because it is a system." This sort of misreading reifies concepts and moves the entire discourse into speculations about causation similar in kind to an explanation for behavior that attributes the behavior to "poor ego strength." Like the ego, the system is nowhere because it does not exist.

Indeed, what is needed instead are some, hopefully few, clear and simple descriptions of what happens in successful therapy. From these descriptions, ideas about how to help patients or clients make changes they will find satisfactory will be derived directly from the actual doing of therapy. With see-through mirrors and videotape, it is now possible to watch successful therapy and it is no longer necessary to depend on the stories of the participants. Therapy needs to be described in such a way that therapists understand what to do and how to do it. Obviously, such a description of what happens in the therapy context needs to be built up out of a series of utterly simple and clear principles.

In theory construction "it's always a matter of the application of a series of utterly simple basic principles and the – enormous – difficulty is only one of applying these in the confusion our language creates. . . . [Interestingly,] the difficulty in applying the simple basic principles shakes our confidence in the principles themselves" (Wittgenstein, 1975a, #133).

* * *

Albert Scheflen (1969a) suggests that "if you search human behavior in a certain way, there is every indication you will find reliable, determined order or pattern in any interaction you examine. The necessary strategies of search are these:

> First, you must agree on a frame of reference. Focus on the *form* of behavior, resisting the temptation at this stage to abstract qualities, as you do in a personality study. Refrain from making black-box inferences about the mental or physiological process that mediate behavior.
> Second, your observations must be *first-hand* and not obtained by directly or indirectly asking the subject; he cannot adequately tell you what he is doing. What he will report are *feelings about* behavior or idiosyncratic or cultural myths about

behavior. Such data are useful in making inferences or studying myth systems but not in determining behavioral pattern [sic].

Third, you must not be satisfied to isolate bits of behavior and merely measure or count them. It is the *relations* of the elements or events, the configuration, the pattern we are after. (pp. 209–210)

For Scheflen (1969b),

there seems to be little value in retaining terms like psyche to represent directly observable behavior. The observable activity of the organism we can call behavior, and reserve the term psyche for a subject's impression of his own and other behavior (i.e., "reality"). We can conclude immediately that most, if not all, of a subject's knowledge of himself and the world has been *learned*. Often, to be sure, it was learned as "insight" from his own observations, but more often it is learned in his family and his culture.

That fact is that members of a cultural tradition learn not only what behavior to perform in a given situation, but what to *say* about it. What one learns to say becomes what one learns to think. It is, therefore, no longer tenable to base psychodynamic models on linear causation and say that thought *causes* behavior. For obviously the two are interconnected in multiple simultaneous causation, together with other aspects of organism state and social situation. (p. 166)

* * *

Lincoln and Guba, in their book *Naturalistic Inquiry* (1985, p. 37), compared the positivist paradigm[4] and what they called the "naturalist paradigm"[5]:

[4]Structural thinking, to be explored in Chapters 3 and 4, seems to fit within a positivist paradigm.

[5]Interactional constructivism and post-structural thinking, the main focus of this book, seems to fit well within Lincoln and Guba's naturalistic paradigm. Their label is unfortunate because it implies that there might be or is an "unnaturalistic paradigm." Therefore, I will drop their terms and use the broader term "post-structural thinking" and the more general distinction between structural and post-structural (see Chapter 5).

Positivist	Naturalist
REALITY is single, tangible, and fragmentable.	REALITIES are multiple, constructed, and holistic.
KNOWER and known are independent, a dualism.	KNOWER and known are interactive, inseparable.
TIME- and CONTEXT-free generalizations are possible.	Only TIME- and CONTEXT-bound working hypotheses are possible.
There are REAL CAUSES, temporally precedent to or simultaneous with their effects.	All entities are in a state of mutual simultaneous shaping, so that it is impossible to distinguish CAUSES from EFFECTS.
Inquiry is value-FREE.	Inquiry is value-BOUND.

Although the above chart is just a list of axioms designed to highlight contrasts and not a full-blown description of both perspectives, Scheflen's view and the view of the therapy situation as a system fit better within Lincoln and Guba's naturalist paradigm[6] than they do within the positivist paradigm.

[6]A full description of the naturalistic paradigm and a detailed comparison with the positivistic paradigm is beyond the scope of the book. The interested reader is urged to read Lincoln and Guba (1985).

3

FROM BOUNDARY TO BARRIER:
Structuralist Thought

Therapists from Sigmund Freud to Salvador Minuchin to Mara Selvini Palazzoli have attempted to derive meaning and understanding by looking behind or underneath what is going on. For Freud, meaning was found in the psyche, in the unconscious, in dreams; for Selvini Palazzoli, meaning was found in the system; and for Minuchin, meaning was found in the "family structure." All are looking for general laws that would provide clues to the meaning of what they observe. In a Kuhnian (1970) sense, family therapy, and indeed the majority of therapy since Freud (and including Freud), seems to exemplify structuralist thought, to fit within a broad structuralist paradigm.

> **structure, 4:** the arrangement or interrelation of all the parts of a whole; manner of organization or construction.
> **structural, 1:** pertaining to structure; having or characterized by structure.

For structuralists, the study of behavior—for instance, of linguistic phenomena—leads to the study of unconscious infrastructures, aimed at discovering general laws (Levi-Strauss, 1963). For instance, there is Chomsky's (1968, 1980) structural view of language with a "surface structure" (the actual words and sentences used) whose meaning is subjective and internally known or derived by a translation process that involves an underlying "deep structure."

> **structural linguistics,** language study based on the assumptions that a language is a coherent system of formal signs and that the task of linguistic study is to inquire into the nature of those signs and their peculiar systematic arrangement.

The work of Bandler and Grinder (1975) is the clearest, most explicit illustration of this usually implicit structuralist thought common to therapeutic discourse.

According to structuralist thought, the meaning of a sign, a word, or any other behavior can be known through its signifier or its deep structure. (Minuchin's "structural family therapy" is but one member of a much larger class known as "structuralism.")

> **structuralism,** a movement for determining and analyzing the basic, relatively stable structural elements of a system, especially in the behavioral sciences.

"The Structuralists, in general, are concerned to *know* the (human) world – to uncover it through detailed observational analysis and to map it out under extended explicatory grids. Their stance is still the traditional scientific stance of Objectivity, their goal the traditional scientific goal of Truth" (Harland, 1987, p. 2). Traditional forms of psychotherapy, including brief psychodynamic therapy and most family therapy, are based on structural thought, on what seems to be a commonsense point of view about problem-solving: Before a problem can be solved or an illness or disease cured, it is necessary to find out what is wrong, to make a diagnosis. That is, they share the structuralist assumption that a rigorous analysis of the problem leads to understanding it and its underlying causation or disease; what the client presents or complains about is ordinarily seen as just a *symptom* of something else. This structuralist idea is, in fact, built into the word "symptom" itself.

symptom, 1: any condition accompanying or resulting from a disease and serving as an aid in diagnosis. **2:** a sign or token; that which indicates the existence or occurrence of something else. *syn.* indication, mark, sign, token

Structuralist thought points to the idea that symptoms are the result of some underlying problem, a psychic or structural problem, such as incongruent hierarchies, covert parental conflicts, low self-esteem, deviant communication, repressed feelings, "dirty games," etc.

As Palazzoli, Cirillo, Selvini, and Sorrentino (1989) put it, describing a point of view not dissimilar to the points of view of many family therapists:

> [We] see the symptom as grounded in three *causative* levels: (a) sociocultural, (b) familial, and (c) individual. The sociocultural level *determines* the special way psychotic malaise will manifest itself during a certain period of history (viz. hysteria in the sexphobic bourgeoisie during the 19th century). The second level, that of family relations will, as long as the family remains the individual's biological and affective matrix, be the *breeding ground* for certain relational patterns that may *usher in* psychotic disorder. The individual level is related to personal traits and circumstances that may *cause* one member of a family rather than another to find himself in an untenable position. (p. 193) [Emphasis added]

Frequently, family therapists also assume that symptoms have beneficial effects or functions, such as preventing something worse from happening, e.g., anorexia is seen as preventing destruction of the family unit. This "benevolent" assumption again leads to the idea that there must be a family problem underlying or creating a situation in which anorexia develops. Based on the logic of these structuralist assumptions, maintaining the problem has something to do with structural difficulties, hierarchical difficulties, intrapsychic difficulties, systemic homeostasis, etc. Given this common bias, that problems are rooted in history and pathology (whether individual or systemic), it is little wonder that therapists frequently think therapy needs to be and should be "long-term." After all, the problem is but the tip of the structural iceberg.

It is generally assumed that therapy focuses on getting rid of these causes in order to solve the problem or cure the illness. Thus, the therapeutic objective encompasses breaking up the problem-maintaining mechanisms. Various models suggest that changing the family structure, altering the family system's homeostatic plateau, correcting the family's hierarchy, strengthening the client's ego, and/or reconstructing the client's personality will lead to a cure[1] or "ease."

(Clients' constructions or beliefs about their problems, although sometimes related in theme and structure, are relatively benign. Perhaps they want to tell therapists the problem's history and their ideas about causation because they think that is what therapists want to hear. They have learned from our Freudian popular culture that therapists think that solving a problem involves *getting at the cause of it* because "stuffing the feelings down" will cause some other, perhaps more serious psychiatric symptoms to arise.)

SYSTEM, FAMILY, FAMILY THERAPY

But what kind of system is being referred to when family therapists use the term? Does it mean more than just the general statement that these therapists use general system theory to guide and organize their thinking? Is it more than just a replacement for psyche?

In the family therapy discourse (reflected in the literature), the terms family and system are often set together (i.e., "the family system") as a symbiotic or mutually defining pair. Some family therapists see and work "with the family as a natural group whose members or acts are related to each other in a mutually responsive way so that we may describe them [the

---

[1]Given these structuralist ideas about family therapy, ideas that explicitly or implicitly seem to put the blame on the family or see the family's structure as causal to the problems, it is little wonder that some consumer groups are openly hostile to "family therapy."

family] as a *system* . . . the conceptual difficulties of viewing them [the family] so [as a system] come from our arbitrary (cultural) assumption that the individual is the 'natural' unit, rather than the group or system" (Beels & Ferber, 1973, p. 206). Many family therapists, for instance Epstein (1988) and Palazzoli (Palazzoli et al., 1989), continue the tradition of setting "family" and "system" together as a way of marking the distinction between family therapy and other kinds of therapy. "The systems model[2] postulates," according to Minuchin, Rosman, and Baker (1978), "that certain types of family organization are closely related to the development and maintenance of psychosomatic syndromes in children, and that the child's psychosomatic symptoms in turn play an important role in maintaining the family homeostasis. Anorexia nervosa is defined not only by the behavior of one family member, but also by the interrelationship of all family members" (p. 21). Here, the family, as equated with "system," is the patient and therefore the target of family therapy's intervention.

However, the therapy situation *seen as a whole* necessarily involves what the therapist and client are doing in the therapy situation together. Reifying the difference between the components of a whole leads to what Wilden describes as "imaginary oppositions"[3] (p. 220). At this point, the methodological boundary around the family as a system, as Wilden (1980) puts it, "denies the relationship [between therapist and client] . . . by splitting wholes into supposedly independent things" (p. 210) and fails to recognize the "impossibility of separating the . . . observer [the therapist] from the observed phenomena" (Capra, 1977, p. 266).

This conceptual violence, "splitting wholes into supposedly independent things," can lead to extreme, violent positions like Palazzoli et al.'s (1989):

[2]"*The* systems model" implies that Minuchin et al. think there is only one "systems model."

[3]The use of "strategy" (Haley, 1963) and "tactics" (Fisch, Weakland, & Segal, 1983), meant to suggest careful planning on the part of the therapist, implies *at the very least* that the therapist and the client are involved in a contest.

We repeatedly came across skillfully concealed games and maneuvers which, in the colloquial language of our team, we came to call "dirty games". . . . A game was "dirty," in our use of the term, when the players resorted to foul means such as subtle cunning, brazen lies, relentless vindictiveness, treachery, manipulation, seduction, ambiguous betrayal, and so on. Such means appeared particularly "dirty" because their real purpose . . . was masked or disavowed. Our hypothesis was that the patient's psychotic behavior was directly linked to a dirty game. We were repeatedly able to confirm this. (pp. 77–78)

dirty, 2: obscene, pornographic. **3:** contemptible, mean.

Palazzoli et al.'s concept of "dirty games" tears the interactive system (the therapeutic situation, a whole) apart, and the resulting imaginary differences lead to a power-oriented relationship involving a certain kind of violence. This converts therapy into a relationship in which the therapist is seen as operating on the family/system and acting "like a 'hunter' [whose] intervention is somewhat like a harpoon" (Palazzoli et al., 1989, p. 243).

To be fair, in a footnote on page 77, Palazzoli et al. claim that their terminology – "dirty games," "hunters with harpoons," etc. – is a matter of convenience and is not meant to heap abuse on people. In a footnote on page 243 they claim that they do not think of families as "fair game" to be gone after with inhumane weapons. Here I would like to point to Einstein's idea that your theory determines what you see, and seeing clients as "skillfully concealing" their dirty games leads to the therapist's needing to hunt down those dirty games using metaphorical harpoons or other violent means to end them.

Can a tongue say "dirty game" while a mind withholds the pejorative and depreciative judgment implied in the label itself? Is Palazzoli not committing herself when she chooses such terms? After all, the word "dirty" automatically carries with it the dictionary definitions and much more, including all of our previous uses of the word. And of course footnotes are usually considered marginal, or at least secondary. Since the footnote is not part of the main text, it is, therefore, not as important (to the author) as that which it footnotes. This secondary status, given by its location on the page itself, undermines the seriousness of Palazzoli et al.'s disclaimer and, therefore, it suggests that what they really meant to say they put into the main text. The disclaiming footnote is only an afterthought.

At this violent extreme,[4] the concept developed from the methodological boundary around the family-seen-as-a-system has outlived its usefulness and needs to be gotten rid of because, once reified, it can never again be a useful metaphor.

* * *

The methodological boundary around the family as a system need not lead to such extremes. While Minuchin et al. (1978) refer to "the anorectic family" and "the psychosomatic family" as entities that can be known as such outside of the therapeutic setting, they nonetheless state that "the systems or family therapist sees himself as very much a member of the therapeutic system" (p. 86). Stierlin and Weber (1989), while referring to "the families of anorectics," are quite clear that "as family researchers and therapists, we are made aware again and again how much we ourselves, via our experience, perception, and evaluation of what we take to be essential and inessential factors, are constituent elements of the resultant image of a given family" (p. 23). For them,

> there is no such thing as a reality independent of the observer. The very process of observing changes what is being observed. . . . The therapeutic context and the relationship between the therapist and the system undergoing treatment are seen as being among the elements shaping the therapeutic process at all times. Hence, in this process the essential thing is to open up or generate realities that increase available alternatives and thus new paths of development (for the individual and the family as a whole). (p. 62)

[4]See also the work of Madanes (Cornille, 1989).

The therapist-as-observer is always already part of the therapeutic context and, as such, is a member of the interactional system. That is, content aside, with any message the question arises, "What sort of message it is to be taken as, and, therefore, ultimately to the *relationship* between the communicants?" (Watzlawick et al., 1967, p. 52). In family therapy, the family or the family seen as a system can only be described in interaction with the therapist.

* * *

In general, we have seen, so far, that some family therapists use the concept of system structurally as equivalent to or as a replacement for the concept of psyche, whereas others use the concept as equivalent to the term family. They are

> concerned with how repetitive sequences reveal and reflect form. Symptoms are seen as serving a function in the family and as carrying metaphorical information about hierarchical dysfunction. Sequences are observed in order to map out a family's organization. (Cade, 1987, p. 38)

These family therapists see the family system or the family structure as the focus of their therapeutic effort. The structure or the hierarchy of the family is seen as the foundation (or cause) of the problems brought to family therapists, and thus the problems or complaints that people talk about to therapists are frequently seen by therapists as metaphors for an underlying dysfunctional system. Inherent in this position is that therapy needs to involve changes in the underlying structure; otherwise change is precarious. That is, the cause of the problem will remain and eventually resurface in the same or some other form.

Some other therapists, as we will see, use the concept of system differently, to refer to the linguistic (verbal and nonverbal) relationships among people. For them

> an analysis of the repetitive sequences surrounding symptoms is a sufficient level of explanation, and inferences about pur-

pose, function, or family structure are seen as unnecessary. Sequences are observed in order to identify self-reinforcing patterns of behavior. (Cade, 1987, p. 38)

These family therapists and brief therapists take what people talk about and how they talk about it at face value, looking at observable behavior and not looking behind or beneath it.

4

LOOKING BEHIND
AND BENEATH:
Structuralist Thought, Brief Therapy

The value of brief treatment modalities has to do with their challenge to the myth that psychotherapy must be of long duration in order to produce behavioral change. The notion that human beings are so rigid, so inflexible, and so unyielding that they require a great deal of time to learn and change is an insult....

—Sifneos, 1990, p. 323

It should come as no surprise that "brief therapy" is another family resemblance concept: It is difficult to define because the distinction between "brief therapy" and "family therapy" and between "brief therapy" and "nonbrief therapy" is so fuzzy.

> **brief, 1:** short; not lasting; ending quickly. **2:** concise; of few words; compact in expression. **3:** short in manner; curt; abrupt. **4:** of limited length or extent; short in length. *syn.* condensed, concise, laconic, short, succinct, curt, transitory.

As a first attempt to read the term "brief therapy," the dictionary points to brevity and also suggests that it might be transitory and limited. The thesaurus points in the same directions, i.e., short, succinct, terse, quick, fleeting.

In a certain sense, brief therapy is neither rare nor unusual. Whether by design or default, therapists can expect one (1) to be the modal number of sessions throughout their career. And, regardless of the therapist's model, one session can be sufficient. For instance, Freud (1960) reports that he cured Gustav Mahler's sexual impotence during a single long walk in the woods. Malan and his associates (Malan, Heath, Bacal, & Balfour, 1975) report studying 45 "untreated neurotic patients" two to nine years after a single "consultation"[1] with no subsequent therapy. A team of psychoanalysts saw 11 of the 45 as being improved symptomatically and in regard to other psychodynamic criteria. The "symptoms" of the patients in this study included depression, anxiety, impotence, frigidity, etc. Furthermore, 22 were seen to have improved "symptomatically" and 10 were seen to be improved "psychodynamically." Perhaps "brief dynamic psychotherapy" is the "essence of analysis" as Gustafson described it (1986, p. 18).

The results of brief therapy, of any type, are often dismissed as "'a transference cure,' 'a counterphobic reaction,' or a 'flight into health'" – all of which Sifneos' colleagues "viewed as being of no therapeutic significance" (Sifneos, 1985, p. 315). This is, of course, a common reading of the term, a way that brief therapy is seen by other, traditional therapists who do not see their therapy as "brief." Except for this chapter, this book focuses on a specific tradition of brief therapy (de Shazer, et al., 1986; Weakland, Fisch, Watzlawick, & Bodin, 1974) that is also subject to this dismissive or disapproving attitude.

THE PSYCHODYNAMIC TRADITION

Various types of psychotherapy and even some types of family therapy, i.e., ones based on psychodynamic ideas, for instance "interpretation of resistance, ambivalence, and negative transference . . . concentrating on interpreting defenses" (Malan, 1976, p. 23), or "unresolved Oedipal interactions" (Sifneos, 1990, p. 320) may last for hundreds of sessions spread over

---

[1]Can a patient be "untreated" if there was one session, even though that was called a "consultation"?

many years (up to four sessions in a week), therefore, "brief therapy" is a relative term.

The various "brief therapies" are all termination-determined activities: some use time constraints, some use goal achievement (the therapist's or the client's goal), and some use both time limits and goal achievement. Within the psychodynamic brief therapy tradition, Malan (1976) limits his work to 40 sessions, Mann (1973) sets a *maximum* of 12 sessions including an absolute date for termination that is set at the beginning, and Strupp (1988) sets a limit at 20 sessions. Although therapy is usually 8 to 14 sessions, Sifneos (1985) no longer sets a limit because therapy can be brought to an early end "when the patient is able to give an example of tangible evidence of behavioral change, or of handling a problem in a different, more adaptive way in contrast to the neurotic way that he used in the past, this should say to the therapist that enough progress has been made" (p. 319).

Each of these models tends to schedule weekly sessions and has stringent client selection criteria such as those developed by Sifneos (1965) and seconded by Mann (1973):

1. Above average intelligence.
2. At least one meaningful relation with another person during the patient's lifetime.
3. An emotional crisis.
4. Ability to interact well with the evaluating psychiatrist and to express feeling.
5. Motivation to work hard during psychotherapy.
6. A specific chief complaint.

Obviously, these criteria[2] potentially limit any model's usefulness in general practice. Most frequently, the problem or complaint is clear-cut and the client in psychodynamic brief therapy is an individual.

---

[2]"Of selection criteria, the only factor that appeared to correlate with favorable outcome was high motivation for insight" (Malan, 1976, p. 20).

SYSTEMIC BRIEF THERAPY

There are, of course, other types of "brief therapy." For instance, in the behavioral tradition, Lazarus and Fay have designed "multimodal brief therapy" (1990) to take 10 to 20 sessions. Simon et al. (1985) draw a distinction between psychoanalytically based brief therapy and systemically oriented brief therapy, which

> developed from the implications of systems theory concepts. An understanding of second-order change has shown that the structure of the system is capable of discontinuous and erratic change. Brief therapy aims at removing the barriers to the development and adaptability of family systems and reinstating the family's potential for self-organization.
>
> In contrast to psychoanalytically based, brief therapy approaches, which of necessity limit themselves to focusing on one problem, systemically oriented, brief therapy methods are not merely "second best." Both cybernetics and systems theory have proven that the self-organizational processes of systems can change in either a continuous or discontinuous manner. In psychoanalytic treatment, change is expected to take place through continuous, not discontinuous, working-through. The success of such change is related to a great extent to the length of treatment, the number of therapy hours, and so on. Systemically oriented procedures, on the other hand, attempt to effect, by means of a few interventions, a second-order or discontinuous change in system patterns in the entire family as well as in each individual family member. . . . Brief therapy consists of a limited number of sessions (usually 6 to 15) spaced at intervals of one to six weeks. . . . The decisive change process often does not take place in their therapy sessions themselves but, rather, in the intervals between sessions. (pp. 28–29)

Systemic brief therapy relates to traditional family therapy in much the same way that brief psychodynamic therapy relates to traditional psychodynamic therapy. The early work of the Milan team (Palazzoli, Boscolo, Cecchin, & Prata, 1978), who limited themselves to 10 sessions in one year, calling their work "long brief therapy," and the brief therapy project at the

Ackerman Institute (Papp, 1983), which was limited to 12 sessions at the start (although the limit to the number of sessions was later dropped) are based on an understanding of systemic therapy that emphasizes the "homeostatic" aspects of systems and the (so-called) function of symptoms. In these and other "systemic" models (brief or long term), "the family is viewed as a self-organizing, cybernetic system in which all the elements are linked to one another, and the presenting problem of the family fulfills a specific function for the family system" (Simon et al., 1985, p. 357).

Although Stierlin and Weber (1989) do not use the label "brief therapy," if we consider just the number of sessions as a way to draw a distinction between "brief therapy" and other nonbrief therapies, their study of the treatment of anorexia nervosa (Stierlin & Weber, 1989), where they limited themselves to 10 sessions per case with four to eight weeks between sessions, should be considered "brief," even though the treatment may last up to two years. They see their work as both "systemic" and "constructivist."[3]

* * *

But, as Beels and Ferber (1973) point out, family therapy is often shorter than individual therapy, and therefore the above description/definition is not quite enough to distinguish types of brief therapy that are related to family therapy from other types of family therapy that are not labeled as "brief." All of the models of brief therapy (both the above and in the next chapter) have one central feature in common: There is a clear-cut way to know when therapy is done, i.e., by counting the number of sessions, by the client's making a significant change and thus reaching the therapeutic goal, and/or by the client's reaching his or her goal for therapy.

---

[3]The term "constructivist" will be left undefined until Chapter 5. It refers, in general, to a philosophic stance vis-à-vis reality, i.e., "There is no such thing as a reality independent of the observer. The very process of observation changes what is being observed" (Stierlin & Weber, 1989, p. 62).

5

JUST SCRATCHING THE SURFACE:

Constructivism, Post-Structuralism, Brief Therapy

"Now," says Wittgenstein, "the only way to escape from the intolerable contradictions involved in such a project is to turn around the whole perspective from which we look at things" (1968, #108). We are not concerned with anything hidden, because everything already "lies open to view" (1968, #126). Instead of penetrating vision, what we want is to command a clear view (1968, #122). It is true that in a sense there is something "hidden," but not because it lies beneath the surface: rather, it is because it is right on the surface, in plain sight (like Poe's purloined letter). "The aspects of things that are most important for us are hidden because of their simplicity and familiarity, (One is unable to notice something—because it is always before one's eyes.)" (1968, #129).

—Staten, 1984, p. 76

REALITIES = LANGUAGE

Ever since *The Invented Reality* (Watzlawick, 1984) and particularly since the *Family Therapy Networker* issue "The Constructivists[1] are Coming" (*Family Therapy Networker*, 1988), there has been a lot of talk about "constructivist therapy," as

---

[1]Although constructivism first appears in the family therapy discourse in the mid-1980s, there is nothing that new about the ideas involved. Ludwig Wittgenstein's mature work started in the 1930s, Jacques Derrida's mature work developed in the late 1960s, de Shazer started "constructing therapeutic realities" in the mid-1970s, and von Glasersfeld (1984b) traces some of the ideas back several centuries.

43

though it were a new school of therapy, a new way of doing therapy. Most typically the use of "constructivism" (as a label for a school of therapy) is based on the verb "construct."

> **construct,** to form by the mind; to originate or invent; as, to construct a plausible story.

Because of Watzlawick's connection to both constructivism and brief therapy, and thus to the concept of reframing,[2] "constructivist therapy" is seen as a version of "brief therapy" or, in a wider framework, involving versions of "strategic[3] therapy." Thus, this usage refers to therapist behaviors, particularly those behaviors some see as manipulative. The root of this usage can be seen in the dictionary and in Roget's *Thesaurus*, where the term "construction" leads to "building, fabricating," etc., and the term "fabricate" leads to "building" and to "invent, make up, trump up, concoct." In the thesaurus in Microsoft Word (a word processing program), "fabricate" leads directly to "concoct, deceive, lie."

In the literature, the term "constructivism" is most frequently used as a label for a point of view, a way of looking at, thinking of, and talking about reality, in other words, epistemology. Reality, or better, realities are invented rather than discovered; humans build the worlds in which they live.

As such, constructivism involves a philosophical point of view, not a theory or model of therapy. If it is to be useful as a frame for looking at therapy, then it needs to be more than the simple slogan: *Reality is invented rather than discovered.* Broadly speaking, therapy looked at from within a constructivist frame only suggests a shared principle: *Reality arises from consensual linguistic processes.* However, as Carlos Sluzki puts it, "once one moves beyond that position it is by no means clear what constructivist therapy entails" (1988, p. 79).

[2]Frames, according to Goffman (1974), are "definitions of a situation [that] are built up in accordance with principles or organization which govern events—at least social ones—and our subjective involvement in them" (p. 10).

[3]that is, therapy that is strategically (Haley, 1963) or tactically (Fisch, Weakland, & Segal, 1983) planned.

Since both doing therapy and talking about therapy involve the use of words, it might be useful to relate constructivism to the broader intellectual context in which it fits, to ideas from 20th-century philosophy of language: structuralism and post-structuralism. To give some rigor to a constructivist approach to looking at therapy, it might be useful to point to some similar ideas that describe realities as arising from linguistic processes. There is no sense in therapists (as amateur philosophers) reinventing an approach to language when philosophers have already done the work for us.

POST-STRUCTURAL THOUGHT

post-, after in time, later, following

In post-structuralist thought, in contrast to structuralist thought, "language constitutes the human world and the human world constitutes the whole world" (Harland, 1987, p. 141). That is, the world is seen *as* language and they [the post-structuralists] doubt the possibility of general laws. With this stance, the post-structuralists invert our standard models of reality and what we used to think of as "surface" or superstructure, as something built upon a structure, actually takes precedence over what we thought of as basic. In post-structuralist thought, our world, our social context, is seen as created by language, by words.

precedence, the act, right, privilege, or fact of preceding in time, place, order, or importance.
invert, 1: to turn upside down. 2: to change to the direct opposite; to reverse the order, position, direction, etc., of.

For the structuralist, meanings are stable and knowable through transformation, but for the post-structuralist, meaning is seen as known through social interaction and negotiation; meaning here is open to view since it lies between people rather than hidden away inside the individual. Thus, if reality is to be seen as invented, as the constructivists say, then constructivism might fit more readily with some sort of post-structural philosophical thought better than it does within structural thought.

> **negotiate, 2:** to hold conference and discussion with a view to reaching agreement . . . ; to treat with another or others respecting . . . any subject of common concern.

Constructivism involves a shift away from objectivism, a shift from discovery to invention (Watzlawick, 1984), and therefore, involves a theory or theories of knowledge, asking the question, "How do we know what we believe we know?" – again, epistemology.

Traditionally, "what we believe we know" has, almost without exception, been understood to refer to the individual's cognitions, which must correspond to reality. Truth or true knowledge was supposed to match with what is real in a world that exists "out there," independent of the observer. However,

> once the cognizing subject is no longer seen as a passive receiver of "information," there is a radical shift of perspective. Perhaps the most dramatic consequence of that shift concerns the concept of "knowledge." Instead of the paradoxical requirement that knowledge should reflect, depict, or somehow correspond to a world as it might be without the knower, knowledge can now be seen as *fitting* the constraints within which the organism's living, operating, and thinking takes place. From that perspective, then, "good" knowledge is the repertoire of ways of acting and/or thinking that enable the cognizing subject to organize, to predict, and even to control the flow of experience. (von Glasersfeld, 1984a, p. 3)

Within the therapeutic context, Von Glasersfeld's radical constructivism (1984a, 1984b), as well as constructivism in general, moves away from objectivity, but this form of constructivism, by itself, retains subjectivity in the form of the cognizing individual as the knower. However, von Glasersfeld's radical constructivism is not radical enough; it seems to draw, once again, the methodological boundary around the client, who is the individual cognizing subject.

* * *

Suppose that you came to me as a client. You can *know* that you are depressed. So far your experience has fit with that idea, that knowledge. Nothing has happened to you to suggest that you are wrong. Your view of yourself fits within the constraints of your environment, allowing you to predict certain things: your response to efforts to cheer you up and other people's response to your being down.

You say to me, "I am depressed." I *know* you *know* that, but I do not know from your statement that you are depressed. The words "depressed" and "depression" are not depression itself. So, given my 20 years of experience, I wonder how you are using that word. I ask, "How do you know you are depressed?" At that point you need to use some criteria, some evidence that will support your knowledge and your use of the word "depressed."

You might say in support of your knowledge that you know you are depressed right now, "Because I've been depressed all my life." However, this undermines and contaminates your statement, "I am depressed," because you might be using the word "depressed" as equivalent to the word "normal." For me, the statement that you've been depressed all your life is no criterion for using the word "depressed"; it is not evidence for being depressed right now because you might have been mistaken all your life. Therefore, I ask, "How do you know that?"

Now you are probably wondering about how you will ever convince me that you are depressed; therefore, you say, "I never get anything done. I either sleep too much or have difficulty sleeping and I either gorge myself or I starve myself." OK, now both you and I are starting to have some ideas about how you are using the word "depressed." We may agree or disagree about your use of that word, we may agree to use some other word(s), or you may continue to use that word while I call it something else.

I might ask, "When was the most recent time when you were not aware that you were depressed?" You search your memory and say, "Oh, last Tuesday." This further contaminates and undermines your use of the words "always depressed" and so sparks my curiosity. I ask, "What did you do last Tuesday?" You say, "I got up early and played golf for the first time in eight months." And I will say, "What else was different on last Tuesday?" "I went out for pizza and beer, danced with a couple of girls, and fell asleep on the couch before I wanted to go to bed." Within the context of this imaginary conversation, we both know that your use of the word "depressed" is different from your criteria for saying that you are not depressed and now we have criteria for both concepts. Together we have constructed a meaning for your use of the word "depressed" that includes (a) *not* playing golf, (b) *not* going out for pizza and beer, (c) *not* dancing with girls, and (d) *not* spontaneously falling asleep on the couch before you are ready for bed. This definition, what we have agreed you mean by your use of the word "depressed," may or may not have been part of the meaning that you brought with you into the session, and it may or may not have been part of the meaning I brought into the session.

* * *

A more radical *interactional* constructivism is needed when the methodological boundary is drawn around the therapeutic situation. A social or interactional theory of knowledge, such as developed by Wittgenstein (Bloor, 1983) and the post-structuralists will prove more useful in describing what is going on within that particular context.

Harland (1987), who sees structuralist thought as concerned with Objectivity and Truth, takes what may be an extreme position and sees post-structural thought as

not only incompatible with the concept of structure but also radically anti-scientific. In effect, the Post-Structuralists bend the philosophical implications of the Superstructuralist way of thinking about superstructures back round against the traditional stance of Objectivity and the traditional goal of Truth. And, with the destruction of Objectivity and Truth, scientific *knowledge* becomes less valuable than literary or political *activity*; and detailed observational analysis and extended explicatory grids are discarded in favor of instantaneous lightning-flashes of paradoxical illumination. (p. 3)

At least "scientific knowledge" is no more and no less valuable than other kinds of knowledge; it is just different. The main difference between scientific knowledge and narrative knowledge is that

scientific knowledge requires that one language game, denotation, be retained and all others be excluded. . . . Drawing a parallel between science and non-scientific (narrative) knowledge helps us understand, or at least sense, that the former's existance is no more – and no less – necessary than the latter's. Both are composed of sets of statements; the statements are "moves" made by the players within the framework of generally applicable rules. . . . It is therefore impossible to judge the existence or validity of narrative knowledge on the basis of scientific knowledge or vice versa: the relevant criteria are different. (Lyotard, 1984, pp. 25–26)

But, don't physicists tell stories about subatomic particles and black holes so that they can let one another know about such things? Are these stories science or narrative?

* * *

Hintikka and Hintikka (1986) describe Wittgenstein as holding a view similar to that of the post-structuralists and assuming that one cannot step outside of one's language to look at one's language and describe it

as one can do to other objects that can be specified, referred to, described, discussed, and theorized about in language . . . one can use language to talk about something only if one can rely on

a given definite interpretation, a given network of meaning relations obtaining between language and the world. Hence one
cannot meaningfully and significantly say in language what
these meaning relations are, for in any attempt to do so one
must already presuppose them. [This is] the gist of this view of
language as the universal medium. (pp. 1–2)

Post-structuralists, in fact, question the opposition of the
subject and the object upon which the possibility of objectivity
depends.

Between, Not Inside

"While structuralism sees truth as being 'behind' or 'within' a
text, post-structuralism stresses the interaction of reader and
text as a productivity" (Sarup, 1989, p. 3). Of interest here is
the work of the deconstructivists,[4] particularly Jacques Derrida (1978) and Paul De Man (1979).

> **deconstruction,** as Goolishian defined the term, "to decon-
> struct means to take apart the interpretive assumptions
> of the system of meaning that you are examining, to
> challenge the interpretive system in such a manner that
> you reveal the assumptions on which the model is based.
> At the same time as these are revealed, you open the
> space for alternative understanding." (Anderson & Gooli-
> shian, 1989, p. 11)

When reading a sentence, the meaning of it is always held in
abeyance and the reader is always waiting for the next word to
help him understand the previous word(s). A later sentence
changes the understanding of an earlier one. There is always
this moratorium on understanding and on meaning because of
the context in which the words are working. The reader brings
to the task of reading all of his previous experiences, all previous uses of the words and concepts, which contaminate what
he reads. For this, the deconstructivists use the term "misread-

---

[4]Notice that "deconstruction" is not the opposite of "construction," whose opposite is "destruction."

ing": Seen in this way, one cannot read, one can only misread. All texts allow for a host of potential misreadings; "There can never be 'objective' interpretation – only more or less vital readings" (Leitch, 1983).

Furthermore, the reader can never know what the author might have meant because he cannot know what the author brought to the meaning of what he wrote. Similarly, the author himself cannot read what he wrote; he too can only misread. Misreading is not a problem to be solved, just a fact to be lived with (De Man, 1979). Rather, each misreading creates a new version of the text and increases both its potential usefulness and potential misunderstanding.

As Richard Harland (1987) puts it, according to Derrida,

> what's in the writer's [user's] mind has no priority over the meaning of his words. On the contrary, the writer [user] only discovers the meaning of his words in the act of writing them. As Derrida, on behalf of all writers, confesses, "before me, the signifier on its own says more than I believe that I meant to say, and in relation to it, my meaning-to-say is submissive rather than active" (Derrida, 1978, p. 178). The written sign [word] is not *sent* but only *received*; even the writer is just another reader. (pp. 131–132)

Wittgenstein (1980) put it this way: "I really do think with my pen, because my head often knows nothing about what my hand is writing" (p. 17).

It is the difference between words that is important. The space between words on the page or the pauses between words while speaking mark the distinction, allowing each word to constrain the meanings of the prior words and subsequent words. Each word, with the meanings brought to it by the reader/author, also opens up the wide range of meanings for the words before and the words after. It is the user's job to pick words that constrain or limit possible misreadings, to restrain meanings from becoming bizarre, to keep things from becoming chaotic.

The work of Wittgenstein and Derrida "converge in the notion of continually different contextualized meanings as the focus of investigation" (Staten, 1984, p. 25). Since a word or a sentence can appear again and again in new contexts where its meaning differs, however slightly, from its meaning in any previous context (even if only because this is now and that was then), in order to understand each appearance in its difference we must study its context (Derrida, 1978). As Henry Staten puts it,

> only in relation to its surroundings in each particular occurrence does the "minimal remainder" that we identify as the same word acquire the charge of differentiation that is required to fill out its "iterated" (repeated yet also transformed, made "other," "iter") sense. (Staten, 1984, p. 25)

However, the distinction between "text" and "context" is difficult to mark. Context is just more text; the meanings of the "context" are just as indeterminable and therefore can produce the same sort of ambiguities. The appeal to context to resolve problematic reading simply moves the problem to another location: It solves nothing.

A BRIEF THERAPY TRADITION

> *The purpose of brief therapy is to influence the client in such a way that his original complaint is resolved to his satisfaction.*
>
> *— Fisch, Weakland, & Segal, 1983, p. 127*

Given the traditional, structuralist assumptions and/or beliefs, brief therapy can seem fundamentally absurd and the reading of the term "brief therapy" suggested by the dictionary (Chapter 4) might seem appropriate. However, this tradition of brief therapy as a constructivist endeavor operates on different assumptions. According to Weakland (1990):

> To make progress toward doing therapy briefly, effectively, and over the widest possible range of problems, we must make a fresh start: in effect, to construct a new myth, a new view of

problems and their resolution that is minimally constrained by past myths. On this view, both practice and thought basically should be exploratory. I see the work of my colleagues and myself at the Brief Therapy Center of MRI . . . and that of Steve de Shazer and his colleagues . . . as exemplifying this view. (Weakland, 1990, p. 107)

Communication theorist Robert Norton (1981) drew the distinction succinctly:

where much of psychiatry spends time trying to unravel the correct, clear cause of the problem with a crystalline analysis devoid of inconsistencies and pure in its structural flow, the brief therapist will settle for a dirty solution that works. The flow of the structure can be marred, illogical, and inconsistent as long as the solution works. (p. 307)

Focused Problem Resolution

As part of a tradition that consciously and deliberately labels itself "brief therapy," Weakland and his associates (Weakland, et al., 1974) at the Mental Research Institute (MRI) set a *limit at 10 sessions* (scheduled weekly) and have found that the average number of sessions it takes to solve the problem is around seven.[5] Both MRI and the Brief Family Therapy Center (BFTC), whose work forms part of the same tradition (see below), have no client selection criteria and thus will work with any clients about any concerns they might have.

The focused problem resolution model of brief therapy (Weakland et al., 1974)

is an out-growth of our earlier work in that it is based on two ideas central to family therapy: (a) focusing on observable behavioral interaction in the present and (b) deliberate intervention to alter the ongoing system. In pursuing these themes further, however, we have arrived at a particular conceptualization

---

[5]When the client uses less than the 10 sessions to solve the problem, the remainder is "left in the bank" for any future need.

of the nature of human problems and their effective resolution, and of related procedures, that is different from much current family therapy. (Weakland et al., 1974, p. 142)

Thus, this tradition of brief therapy is akin to, but distinct in some important ways from, family therapy. Weakland et al. (1974) continue drawing this distinction between brief therapy and family therapy with their conceptualization of human problems and their resolution:

Our fundamental premise is that regardless of their basic origins and etiology – if, indeed, these can ever be reliably determined – the kinds of problems people bring to psychotherapists *persist* only if they are maintained by ongoing current behavior of the patient and others with whom he interacts. Correspondingly, if such problem-maintaining behavior is appropriately changed or eliminated, the problem will be resolved or vanish, regardless of its nature, origin, or duration. (pp. 144–145)

This involves a radical inversion: Where family therapy seems to want to change the underlying system, to look behind and beneath, brief therapy, according to Weakland et al. (1974), is only interested in what is open to view: the surface, the actual, observable, behavioral interaction.

Family therapy also has promoted greater activity by therapists. Once family interaction was seen as significant for problems, it followed that the therapist should aim to change the ongoing system. Extending this, we now see the therapist's primary task as one of taking deliberate action to alter poorly functioning patterns of interaction as powerfully, effectively, and efficiently as possible. (p. 145)

Watzlawick et al. (1974) developed a constructivist concept which they call "reframing"

reframing, to change the conceptual and/or emotional setting or viewpoint in relation to which a situation is experienced and to place it in another frame which fits the

"facts" of the same situation equally well or even better,
and thereby changes its entire meaning. (p. 95)

Although the facts of the situation are not seen as changed
in any way, the context in which they lie is described from a
different observational point of view. The "effect" of this reposi-
tioning or mutation ("change") is seen in reported changes of
behaviors, perceptions, emotional states, and/or beliefs. "Once
they 'see things differently,' they can behave differently" (de
Shazer, 1982a).

The MRI version of constructivism seems to retain the
methodological boundary between therapist and client, between subject and object common to most versions/models of
therapy. Where the structural view assumes that clients' problems are a reflection of a wrong or dysfunctional social organization and intervention is based on a map of what is supposedly a correct family hierarchy, the focused problem-solving
model assumes that clients are doing the best they can and
further assumes that family hierarchy or structure is not important to doing therapy. They do not assume a pathological,
illness, or disease-oriented view of the family or family structure, but rather focus on sequences of interaction and problem-
solving behavior.

The general interactional view developed at MRI (Watzlawick & Weakland, 1977) is built around the idea that relationships can be described as though they follow rules and that
what is going on in the here-and-now of the therapy session, the
patterns of interaction, is vastly more important to effective
therapy than any causal explanations.

By 1968, when the Brief Therapy Center was formed at
MRI, any remnants of structural thought implicit in the double bind theory had gone by the wayside. The brief therapists
at MRI developed the idea that the problems clients bring to
therapists are situational difficulties between people – problems of interaction – and that "once a difficulty begins to be
seen as a 'problem,' the continuation, and often the exacerba-
tion, of this problem results from the creation of a positive
feedback loop, most often centering around those very behav-

iors of the individuals in the system that are intended to resolve the difficulty: The original difficulty is met with an attempted [and failed] solution that intensifies the original difficulty" (Weakland et al., 1974, p. 149). Consequently, "we try to
base our conceptions and our interventions on direct observation in the treatment situation of *what* is going on in systems
of human interaction, *how* they continue to function in such
ways, and *how* they may be altered most effectively" (p. 150).
Thus, for Weakland et al., the system-under-consideration involves the client or clients and their interaction with the problem as depicted in the therapy session.

They describe therapist activity in interaction with the client
as influencing the client during the therapy session: "Once we
[the therapists] have formed a picture of current behavior central
to the problem and estimated what different behavior would lead
to the specific goal selected, the task is one of intervening to
promote such change" (Weakland et al., 1974, p. 155). Thus, the
therapist engages in directing behavioral change, frequently
through paradoxical instructions based on counter or "therapeutic double binds" (Bateson et al., 1956; Watzlawick et al., 1967):
"Such instructions probably constitute the most important single class of interventions in our treatment" (p. 158).

Since the boundary around the system-under-consideration
is traditional – it is drawn around the client-and-problem, thus
separating that system from the therapist and his team behind
the see-through mirror – imaginary oppositions develop, and
the therapist needs to maintain maneuverability and develop
tactics (Fisch et al., 1983). Therefore, focused problem-solving,
although rejecting structuralist thought, retains the boundary
between therapist and client and the subject-object split of
traditional therapy. As such, the work of the brief therapists at
MRI can be seen as transitional, as fitting into a position between structuralism and post-structuralism.

Focused Solution Development

By 1978, the radical shift in perspective from structuralism
to post-structuralism was well underway at the Brief Family

Therapy Center.[6] Rather than draw a boundary around the client-plus-problem as the unit of analysis, and thus a boundary between client and therapist, the boundary was drawn around the client-plus-problem-plus-therapist-plus-team as the system-under-consideration (de Shazer, 1982a, 1982b; Nunnally, de Shazer, Lipchik, & Berg, 1986). Of course, not all of the implications of this mutation or restructuring of the boundary were readily apparent; however, almost immediately, system-wide cooperation was deemed central to effective therapy and thus the "death of resistance" (de Shazer, 1984). Therapeutic change was seen to develop out of the interaction within the therapeutic system itself, as the split between subject and object was rejected.

By 1982, some of the implications of the post-structuralist perspective were becoming more obvious and thus more explicit. Out of our belief that, if therapists accept the client's complaint as the reason for *starting* therapy, therapists should, by the same logic, accept the client's statement of satisfactory improvement as the reason for *terminating* therapy, the idea developed that the client's goals and solutions were more important than the problems the client depicted in the session. This led us to be able to draw a radical distinction between solutions and problems[7] (de Shazer, 1985) and thus to redefine the unit of analysis as involving client-plus-therapist-plus-goal (or solution)-plus-team. That is, solution-focused therapy is seen as a mutual endeavor involving therapists and clients together constructing a mutually agreed upon goal.

At BFTC (de Shazer, 1985, 1988; de Shazer et al., 1986) no limit is set on the number of sessions, and the average number of sessions per case is 4.7. Therapy ends when the client(s) meets his or her or their goal(s) for therapy. At BFTC the interval between sessions increases after the second session, which is usually one week following the first session. Each session is

---

[6]The traditional boundary between client and therapist frames some, but not all, of de Shazer's early work (de Shazer, 1974, 1975).

[7]This point of view was "forced on us" as the only reasonable way to interpret the results of a research project (de Shazer, 1985).

viewed as potentially the last, and even single sessions are looked upon as sufficient therapy provided the client's goal is met to his or her satisfaction.

The focused problem resolution model (Weakland et al., 1974) focuses on interactional sequences in the present. It is aimed at describing attempted solutions that failed, i.e., efforts that are accidently maintaining the problem, and it attempts to intervene to stop those efforts. The focused solution development model, which is related to and yet distinct from the focused problem resolution model, also focuses on interactional sequences in the present and is aimed at describing exceptions to the rule of the complaint and prototypes or precursors of the solution that the client has overlooked, thus intervening to help the client do more of what has already worked.

Problems are seen to maintain themselves simply because they maintain themselves and because clients depict the problem as *always happening*. Therefore, times when the complaint is absent are dismissed as trivial by the client or even remain completely unseen, hidden from the client's view. Nothing is actually hidden, but although these exceptions are open to view, they are not seen by the client as differences that make a difference. For the client, the problem is seen as primary (and the exceptions, if seen at all, are seen as secondary), while for therapists the exceptions are seen as primary; interventions are meant to help clients make a similar inversion, which will lead to the development of a solution.

The focused solution development model of brief therapy actively focuses on the clinical situation that includes both therapist and client, i.e., the methodological boundary is drawn around the therapy-situation-as-a-system, denying the subject-object opposition. De Shazer (1982a, 1982b, 1985, 1988) and his colleagues developed an interactional constructivist, poststructural concept called "cooperation":

> Each family (individual or couple) shows a unique way of attempting to cooperate, and the therapist's job becomes, first, to describe that particular manner to himself that the family

shows and, then, to cooperate with the family's way and, thus, to promote change. (de Shazer, 1982a, pp. 9–10)

How the client depicts his situation or constructs reality and what actually happens in the session are accepted by the therapist at face value and adapted to and utilized by the therapist as the foundation of therapy. This model of solution-determined brief therapy[8] focuses "right from the start of the session on what the client [is] already doing that works. . . . The therapeutic task, when constructed in this way, allows the therapist to readily develop an intervention that fits since the intervention just asks the client to continue to do something. This process of solution development can be summed up as helping an unrecognized difference become a difference that makes a difference" (de Shazer, 1988, pp. 9–10).

* * *

Solution-focused brief therapy will be explored in the subsequent chapters. The above just sets the context in which this approach developed or evolved.

[8]See Appendix 1.

Part Two

6

WHAT IS IN A NAME?
Case Example One: Part One

Language is what bewitches but language is what we must stay within in order to cure the bewitchment.

—Staten, 1984, p. 91

Humpty Dumpty was dead wrong when he said, "When *I* use a word . . . it means just what I choose it to mean—neither more nor less." "The question is," said Alice, "whether you can make words mean so many different things" (Carroll, 1972, p. 90). And Humpty Dumpty was quite right when he continued, "The question is . . . which is to be master—that's all" (Carroll, 1972, p. 90). And the answer is, it is the word that is master. A word always means more and less than we mean it to mean.

*   *   *

WHAT IS GOING ON HERE?

A woman and her husband came to therapy because, six weeks earlier, she had suddenly developed an "insatiable" desire for sex; she had become, in her words, a nymphomaniac.

> **nymphomania,** excessive and uncontrollable sexual desire in the female. from the Greek, *nymphe*, bride, and *mania*, madness.

During this six week period, she had felt that she had to have sexual intercourse at least once a day before going to sleep.

Prior to this session she had been able to restrain herself for two nights in a row by sleeping, fully clothed, on top of the blankets.

The therapist[1] attempted to use these exceptional nights to begin deconstructing the situation, to begin to induce some doubt about the woman's construction of her complaint. That is, the therapist tried to misunderstand these nights with exceptional behavior as exceptions to the complaint itself. (Complaint here is seen to involve both behaviors and what those behaviors mean.) But the woman would have none of it and the negotiation continued. If her only choice was to coercively restrain herself from sex, then, to her this meant that her marriage was no good.

The therapist continued to search for some element of the client's complaint – either in the behavioral elements or in the meanings involved – that could be used as a focal point, a point where the complaint included some undecidable element that could be used to begin constructing a solution. However, the client's description of the complaint went from bad to worse. She wanted normal sex (about three times per week) that was uncontaminated by compulsion. She wanted to just go to sleep without having to have sexual intercourse first. Without her daily "fix" of sex, she was unable to get to sleep. As she saw it, she was having sex for all the wrong reasons; her nymphomania was a problem rooted in her infancy that would require deep therapy.

The negotiations about what was going on switched to her husband, who described her agony about the nymphomania and his tiredness. As he saw it, he was being robbed of the opportunity to be romantic toward her; rather than her lover, he had become just a stud.

> Husband: But for me, it's more of a sleep problem for both
> of us.

[1] Insoo Kim Berg

Therapist: I wonder about that. Maybe we've been looking at this the wrong way.

Wife: Do you have any cures for insomnia?

Therapist: I don't know. We've been looking at this as a sex disturbance, but it's beginning to look more like a sleep disturbance.

The husband's view—his misunderstanding of the situation—once accepted by his wife and the therapist, meant that the negotiations about the complaint could stop, allowing the therapist and the client to cooperate in the construction of a solution.

> **insomnia,** prolonged or abnormal inability to sleep. from the Latin *in*, not, and *somnis*, sleep.

Now the complaint itself has become undecidable: The behaviors have at least two sets of possible meanings (which neither the dictionary nor diagnostic manuals can relate to each other):

1. They might be a sexual disturbance (with sleep disturbance attached), or
2. They might be a sleep disturbance (with sexual disturbance attached).

In addition, other meanings are also possible:

3. Since both happen in bed, they might be seen as related disturbances through the bed-as-context[2] (de Shazer, 1988), or

[2]At the Brief Family Therapy Center these two complaints could be related to each other since both involve the "bed-as-context" (de Shazer, 1988). Seeing the situation this way, an intervention would be built around having the couple swap sides of the bed or to change the location of the bed in the bedroom. However, late in the session when the therapist asked, the couple reported no difference when they changed sides of the bed and the recent redecoration of the bedroom involved changing the position of the bed, but they saw no difference in the complaint.

4. They might, in fact, be some other sort of utterly different disturbance (with sexual and sleep disturbances attached).

As they started to talk about the sleep problem, the woman realized that both the "sex problem" and the "sleep problem" had begun at the time she started to have scheduled and structured exercise for one hour a day every day of the week. Could this be an exercise problem? *At this point in the session, the meaning(s) of what was going on was set adrift in a sea of potential meanings.*

The therapist started to ask questions about sleep and nonsleep, looking for times when the woman went to sleep normally and naturally without first having had sex. Perhaps a model for getting to sleep normally could be found within the client's recent experience. There were some rare and unclear exceptions but both husband and wife dismissed these as flukes.

As the conversation continued, it became clear that the "sleep-problem" label for her complaint was not carrying around the highly pathological meanings she had for the "sex-problem." Since the client accepted this new name for her complaint, the therapist focused the conversation around the difficulties with getting to sleep and emphasized the fact that some sleep disturbance now and then was quite normal. (It is, of course, easier to develop a solution to a "normal difficulty" than it is to develop a solution to a "very pathological problem that has roots deep in my infancy.")

Of course the therapist cannot just pick a new meaning or a new label at random. The new meaning must fit (de Shazer, 1985) within the context, within the pattern of the conversation. In this particular context, fit was a simple matter because the new name for the complaint simply gave precedence to what was seen as secondary (the sleep disturbance) over what had been seen as primary (the sexual disturbance); this is a move typical of post-structural thinking and deconstructivist endeavors.

Throughout the remainder of the session, the therapist kept the conversation strictly on a behavioral level and avoided any further discussion of thoughts, feelings, and meanings. The sleep-disturbance complaint became solely a "behavioral" or "technical" difficulty to be resolved through technical means.

After consulting with the team[3] behind the see-through mirror, the therapist told the woman about some options:

1. Perhaps as an experiment, she could quit exercising for now; or
2. (a) if she found herself awake one hour after going to bed, she was to get up and do hateful household chores, like oven cleaning; or
   (b) if she found herself awake one hour after going to bed, she was to continue to lie there but with her eyes wide open, concentrating on keeping her tongue from touching the roof of her mouth.[4]

After the evening meal, sometime before he went to bed, her husband was to toss a coin to decide whether she was to use (a) or (b) on any particular night.

Two weeks after this session, the woman sent a note thanking the therapist and the team for seeing that her "insatiable need for sex" was but "a symptom of her insomnia." She wrote that "immediately my sleep patterns and my libido returned to normal." She did not say whether she and her husband ever tried the team's suggestions. Perhaps the new name, with its attached meanings, was enough to solve the client's problem and the suggestions were unnecessary.

Therapeutic Misunderstanding

Words are like freight engines that are pulling boxcars behind them filled with all their previous meanings.

In order to present the sense of words we must present the scenes of their use; and these scenes are themselves presented in

---

[3]Steve de Shazer, Larry Hopwood and Jane Kashnig

[4]These are both traditional brief therapy interventions that might be useful when the client complains of "insomnia."

words; the words *are* scenes when their materiality and power of figuration are unleashed. Derrida and Wittgenstein both rely heavily, though in very different ways, on figuration, on image and metaphor, in general on *style*. (Staten, 1984, p. 26)

When the client uses a word – nymphomania – she brings to this particular use all the previous meanings that word has had for her. When you, as reader, read the word "nymphomania," like therapist and team when they hear the word, you bring with you into this specific context all the previous meanings that word has had for you. The therapist "seeks to find the element in the system studied [their conversation about the client's complaint, goals, etc.] which is alogical, the thread . . . which will unravel it all, or the loose stone which will pull down the whole building" (Miller, 1976, p. 341).

Now, you, as reader, cannot know that what the word "nymphomania" means to you right now is what it meant to you 24 hours ago, and you cannot know that 24 hours from now "nymphomania" will mean the same thing to you that it means now. As the author of this piece, I am in no better a position. Obviously, then, within the context of writing and reading, misunderstanding is more likely than understanding.

In face-to-face conversation there is at least the opportunity to negotiate with one another about which meaning of "nymphomania" we are going to use. But in conversation I can, and frequently do, assume that you and I mean the same thing by a particular word; and you can, and frequently do, make the same assumption. Given the many, many possible meanings for the word "nymphomania," or any other word, it is most probable that we will misunderstand.

The therapy system can be seen as a set of "language games," a self-contained linguistic system that creates meanings through negotiation between therapist and client (see Chapter 7). What a therapist and client do during the interview is akin to writing or coauthoring and reading a text. What the rest of the team behind the see-through mirror does is akin to reading a text. When working solo, the therapist needs to do this by herself when thinking about the interview. Thus, a ther-

apeutic interview is a putting together of various misunder-
standings (misreadings) and whatever is meant is a result of
how therapist and client agree to misunderstand (or misread)
what is said: "Nymphomania" becomes misunderstood as "insomnia." The secondary becomes primary and the primary becomes secondary, and the misreading becomes useful to the
client. Again, following Wittgenstein, we can only know what a
word means by how the participants in the conversation use it.

In the therapy situation, metaphorically following the second law of thermodynamics, misunderstanding (chaos) is much
more likely than understanding (order), and perhaps the best
that therapists can do is creatively misunderstand what clients
say so that the more useful, more beneficial meanings of their
words are the ones chosen. Thus, creative misunderstanding
allows the therapist and the client to together construct a reality that is more satisfactory to the client.

It seems that the above case fits within the post-structural
discourse where reality and meaning are developed through
negotiation and not discovered or uncovered by searching for
general laws and unconscious structures. Viewing therapy from
within this framework, both Freud and Minuchin can be seen
as structuralists (they both look for meaning in an underlying
structure; for Freud, the psyche and for Minuchin, the family
structure); on the other hand, Insoo Kim Berg's deconstructing
nymphomania can be seen as both constructivist and post-
structural, but certainly not structural.

* * *

Borders between concepts cannot be depended upon; and
the focus on insomnia during the interview and in the intervention message at the end of the session is designed to impose an
external constraint, an attempt to arrest the slippage of meanings for the purposes of a solution-focused language game.

The change or transformation that follows the redistribution
or inversion of concept and criteria, the reversal of the hierarchy, and the solution-focused language game needs to be held
in place, to be tacked down, within the therapeutic conversa-

tion for pragmatic, therapeutic purposes. Otherwise, the new unstable meaning can continue to slip and slide and the client can "relapse" to nymphomania. Were the slipping and sliding of meaning to continue *ad infinitum* it would, in fact, "leave the field untouched, leaving one no hold on the previous opposition [or difference], thereby preventing any means of *intervening* in the field effectively" (Derrida, 1971, p. 41). The problematic language game would be left intact. Without the intervention, if the term "insomnia" was not tacked down as part of the solution-developing language game, "insomnia" could easily slip back into a problem-focused language game and then "insomnia" might become the name of a substituted "symptom."

Behaving as if meaning were stable seems to be useful in day-to-day life; this is how we normally behave. And any intervention is designed to help the client begin to have new experiences in his or her day-to-day life.

7

LANGUAGE GAMES, SYSTEM
Case Example One: Part Two

In contrast to post-structuralists, structuralists assume that, at least for native speakers of the language, the surface structure can be translated – transformed to and derived from the underlying deep structure or unconscious – and, therefore, there is one true meaning for any concept, whether that concept is "nymphomania" or "dog." (Of course, an individual can use the word wrong or use the wrong word.) "Dog" refers to certain kinds of canines and not other kinds of canines ("wolf"). "Dog" certainly cannot slip over into "cat." Similarly, "nymphomania" means "a sexual compulsion in the female" and not a "sexual compulsion in the male" and not some other sexual problem a female might experience. Within a structural framework, "nymphomania" certainly cannot slip over into "insomnia."

Wittgenstein, however, points out that the meaning of words is determined by how they are used by the various participants within a specific context. There might be a specific context (a language game) in which "dog" can slip over into "cat," for example, when talking about four-legged house pets. Similarly, in a solution-developing language game, "nymphomania" slips over into "insomnia" and then both slip over into "a result of daily exercise." Within this context, nymphomania no longer means a sexual compulsion of a female but refers to another sign; it means "insomnia," which no longer means a "sleep disturbance" but refers back to "nymphomania." Both, furthermore, mean "daily exercise," which does not mean something about physical fitness, but instead means nymphomania and insomnia.

For post-structuralists, signs or words or concepts are seen to float or slide: A sign or a concept simply means (or refers to) another sign or concept. "Dog" is clearly different from "cat," but the border between the two is not guaranteed. That is, in a particular context their meanings float and slide – "dog" may well refer to "cat" and both may mean "house pets" or "meat." "Nymphomania" is clearly marked by its spelling as different from "insomnia," but, as the case example shows, the border between them is not guaranteed; nor is the border between them and "daily exercise" fixed. Derrida points out that borders cannot be depended upon; the focus on insomnia during the interview and in the intervention at the end of the session is designed to impose an external constraint, an attempt to arrest the slippage of meanings. The change or transformation brought about by the inversion of concept and criteria, the reversal of the hierarchy, needs to be held in place for pragmatic, therapeutic purposes. The name of the problem is now "insomnia" (meaning whatever it meant to the couple) and from that a solution somehow developed, a "new more satisfactory life began," involving the whole package of meaning dragged along by ending the insomnia – importantly including the end of the "nymphomania."

*   *   *

One way of conceptualizing and describing the system involved in doing therapy is to use a framework developed by Ludwig Wittgenstein and to look at doing therapy as an example of an activity involving a set of related, but distinct "language games" (Wittgenstein, 1958). "The term 'language game' is meant to bring into prominence the fact that the speaking of language is part of an activity, or of a form of life" (Wittgenstein, 1968, #7). A language game[1] is an activity seen as a

---

[1] We learn games and the foundation of this learning is training, not rule following. With training, while playing a game – as Wittgenstein puts it – we follow rules blindly (not consciously and not deliberately), as a river follows the river bed.

language complete in itself, a complete system of human communication.[2] Language games are complete in the sense that, you've got what you've got and that's all there is. There is no need to look behind or beneath since everything you need is readily available and open to view. Nothing is hidden.

Language games are culturally shared and structured activities that center on people's uses of language to describe, explain, and justify. Language games are activities through which social realities and relationships are constructed and maintained. The signs (or moves) during the game consist of sentences (or signs), which are made up of words, gestures, facial expressions, postures, thoughts, etc. Since this is a system complete in itself, any particular sign can only be understood within the context of the pattern of the activities involved. Thus, the meaning of any one word depends entirely on how the participants in the language game use that word. If the context were significantly different, that game would not be played; it would be a different game altogether.

"Just as a move in chess doesn't consist simply in moving a piece in such-and-such a way on the board—nor yet in one's thoughts and feelings as one makes the move: but in the circumstances that we call 'playing a game of chess'" (Wittgenstein, 1958, #33), so pointing and naming, and understanding such gestures, are not meaningful as such, nor by virtue of some mental act or process that accompanies them. Rather, they are inscribed in a sequence and derive their meaning from a "before" and an "after." There are "characteristic experiences" which accompany our acts of pointing and intending, but these may be absent. And whether these experiences are present or absent, the *meaning* of the gesture would remain independent of them: "It would still depend on the circumstances—that is, on what happened before and after the pointing" (Wittgenstein, 1958, #35). (Staten, 1984, p. 72)

---

[2]In fact, family therapy might be seen as a language game because both writing and talking about it involve "sense making habits and conventions which enable language to perform its various legitimate functions in the world" (Norris, 1983, p. 36).

Hans Fischer (1987) describes the methodological function of language games

> to be a line of investigation or a point of view. It focuses on a smaller unit (language-game) that can be easily overlooked, and thus makes it possible to analyze the mechanism of language without battling against the fog of the entire language system. (p. 171)

The therapeutic relationship is a negotiated, consensual, and cooperative endeavor in which the solution-focused therapist and client jointly produce various language games focused on (a) exceptions, (b) goals, and (c) solutions (de Shazer, 1985, 1988). All of these are negotiated and produced as therapists and clients misunderstand together, make sense of, and give meaning to otherwise ambiguous events, feelings, and relationships. In doing so, therapists and clients jointly assign meaning to aspects of clients' lives and justify actions intended to develop a solution.

*   *   *

At times, Wittgenstein seems to deny "private language" — an argument aimed at introspective psychology and behaviorism. Certainly the woman can *know* that she is a nymphomaniac. However, her saying that she is a nymphomaniac is not identical with her having "nymphomania" or "being a nymphomaniac." But to tell others about it, she needs to put the behavior into language where "outside" criteria are needed for others to understand her. And, as was shown in the previous chapter, these criteria can be used to deconstruct her concept of herself as a nymphomaniac.

This use of the "notion 'language-game,' with all its implications, turns out to be an instrument of a methodologically behavioristic psychology of 'inner states'" (Fischer, 1987, p. 171), where "an 'inner process' stands in need of outward criteria" (Wittgenstein, 1968, #580) in order for the people involved in a language game to jointly arrive at meaning.

According to Fischer, "Wittgenstein is an advocate of methodological behaviorism, as far as the language-game concept is concerned; but outward criteria form the basis for the usage of mental predicates with regard to other persons. The position is methodologically behavioristic; for it does not deny 'inner process,' but shows that our language about mental states presupposes their very existence" (1987, p. 172).

Wittgenstein is not saying that private experiences do not exist. He is merely saying that we need a public framework, a language game, to give meaning to our talk about sensations and other private experiences. Wittgenstein only says that we cannot speak about private experiences without a public framework, without a language game.

* * *

This view of therapy as an activity involving several language games is related to an orientation toward words similar to that described by Mehan and Wills (1988) as "dialogic orientation." They state that

> the idea of competing over the meaning of ambiguous events rests on a view of language that can be understood by visualizing words in a territory or a conversational space. If one conceptualizes conversational space in a personal sense, then one concludes that individuals own meaning, own the territory. Meanings are privately assembled by a solitary speaker and transmitted to a passively receptive hearer. . . . If one conceptualizes words in a dialogic sense, . . . then one concludes the territory is jointly owned. . . . From the dialogic point of view, meaning is neither *in* the speaker or *in* the hearer; it is *in-between* both addressor and addressee. . . . (p. 364)

Thus, as we have seen in the previous chapter, the meaning of the term nymphomania or of any other word/concept depends upon what happens in the interview. The woman and her husband brought a set of meanings for the problem called nymphomania with them into the session, so did the therapist and the team — as did you, the reader, on the first mention of the word. But as the conversation developed, the meaning of the term changed: One of the woman's definitional criteria for the word/concept nymphomania, one of the meanings it held for her—insomnia—became the new name for the problem. That is, what was a secondary or supplemental criterion became primary: Through negotiation nymphomania became but a criterion of insomnia.

Language games, as whole and complete systems of human communication, can be understood as systems of shared meaning and shared behavior. It is in these language games that words, gestures, etc., take on or acquire their meanings. Methodologically, language games, within the activity known as "doing therapy," are the "system" most available to study, in order to understand what therapy is all about. It is language games that serve as boundaries around the possibilities of meanings and as the boundary against nonsense.

INTERACTIONAL CONSTRUCTIVISM OR GENERAL ATTRIBUTES OF A SYSTEM

An observer can see the therapist and client behaving as if they are following rules as they talk together. The observer's describing these rules or the language game's grammar depends on knowing what kind of activity or language game is going on. A goal-setting language game involves a different logic, a different grammar than one that focuses on problem definition. This grammer defines what kind of language game is going on. According to Wittgenstein, "grammar is not accountable to any reality. It is grammatical rules that determine meaning (constitute it) and so they themselves are not answerable to any meaning and to that extent are arbitrary" (1975b, p. 180).

This language system, the communication between therapist and client, has attributes similar to those of any other system (see Chapter 2).

* * *

Wholeness

According to Wilden (1980),

> Concepts . . . are purely differential. They are not defined posi-
> tively by their content, but negatively by their relationship with
> the other terms of the system. Their most exact characteristic is
> to be what others are not. (p. 225)

The concept "N," nymphomania-with-its-criterion-insomnia, is
quite different from the concept "I," insonmia-with-its-criterion-
nymphomania. Clearly, one concept is what the other is not.
Were the meaning of concept N just *inside* the woman (given
nymphomania there must necessarily be some deeper, *underlying pathology)*, the inversion from N to I would not have been
possible since the meanings would not be subject to negotiation. And this difference between N and I seems to make a
difference both to the therapeutic conversation and the woman's reported changes, and to the unmentioned changes that
necessarily follow between the woman and her husband: He
can, once again, be her lover and not just engage in sex in order
to meet her compulsive need.

Of course the inversion, the shift from concept N to concept
I, involves a change in the relationship between nymphomania
and insomnia; a change in the relationship between the therapist and the couple (wife plus husband) and between the woman
and the man; and a change in spouses, from seeing themselves
as helpless in the face of nymphomania (given their meanings)
to seeing themselves as a couple who would use a technical
means to solve the insomnia.

Nonsummativity

By the end of the conversation, each of the concepts N and I
is certainly different from the other. Adding the two concepts
together, [N + I] only leads to ambiguity. Nobody – therapist,
client, author, or reader – would have known what was going on
in this conversation. This ambiguity was resolved by the thera-

pist and client negotiating and between them deciding that this problem was the sort of problem that could be solved through technical means appropriate to a sleep disturbance.[3]

Equifinality, Multifinality

Obviously, if the therapist and the client had been unable to negotiate the inversion of the two concepts, the interview would have taken a different one of the possible paths of the labyrinth; perhaps the ambiguity would have remained the meaning of the whole conversation, perhaps only nymphomania with its criteria would have been the topic or theme of the whole conversation. The meanings initially brought into the session by the therapist, the wife, and the husband did not determine the course of the conversation or how the session ended. Even the therapist's inversion did not determine the rest of the session and, perhaps, even the fact that the shift was accepted by the clients did not necessarily determine the end-state. Perhaps even the session as a whole did not determine what happened in life outside the therapy room that prompted the woman to write of the successful resolution of the problem.

If we draw a line and say that the ending of the conversation with some suggestions is an end-state, then clearly all sorts of different initial conditions or initial states could lead to the therapist and team giving the same suggestions. For those suggestions (if not asleep in one hour (a) do something unpleasant, and/or (b) keep your eyes open and your tongue from the roof of your mouth), only some complaint about some sort of sleep difficulty is required. Just looking at the final message would not begin to suggest the paths that led up to that specific message.

---

[3]If the ambiguity remained at the end of the session, the closing message would have spelled out this ambiguity in detail and ended with a statement similar to this: "We don't know what you are going to do . . . first" (de Shazer, 1985, p. 52). In this way, implying that the client(s) *doing* something would at least solve the ambiguity if not lead to solution.

If we draw the line marking the end-point with the letter from the client reporting the resolution of the problem, there is nothing about the therapeutic conversation that necessarily determines that outcome. Perhaps something else happened between the end of the session and the writing of the letter that prompted her to say that the problem was resolved: Whatever happened (X) might have happened with or without the therapy session. We cannot know if it was the session alone, the session plus X, or X alone that prompted the resolution. All we can know about is the session itself and the letter itself: In the letter she attributes the resolution and success to the therapy.

Circular Causality, Nonlinearity

In systems, there is no such thing as simple, linear cause-effect relationships. We cannot know which one of the events (described in our description of the conversation) "caused" the solution to the problem; we cannot know if the whole sequence of events "caused" the solution; we cannot know if eliminating one of the events or a different order of events might have made a difference; we cannot know if some perhaps hypothetical event outside of therapy with or without the conversation "caused" the solution, etc.

We've got what we've got and that's all there is. The whole of the "system," this activity with its particular language games, is its own best ~~explanation~~ or description. (Throughout the book, this sort of strikethrough indicates a word used but not quite meant. "The idea is this: Since the word is inaccurate, or rather, inadequate, it is crossed out. Since it is necessary it remains legible" (Sarup, 1989, p. 35). No other word will quite do the trick. This device is derived from the work of Martin Heidegger.)

We can describe what happened and we can even watch a videotape of the session and read the letter, but we cannot know what "caused" the solution and, in that sense, there can be no explanation, no accounting for it. We cannot state reasons for what happened, we cannot look behind or beneath; beyond description, we can only speculate.

Perhaps, then, we ought to put the concept of ~~cause~~ or ~~causality~~ on hold. Perhaps we ought to make a Wittgensteinian move and say that, since we cannot know about causation, we might as well pretend that it does not exist and see what happens.

ꞌ

8

THE CONCEPT OF ~~PROBLEM~~[1] EXCEPTION

Case Examples Two and Three

Now, patients that come to you, come to you because they don't know exactly why they come. They have problems, and if they knew what they were they wouldn't have come. And since they don't know what their problems really are, they can't tell you. They can only tell you a rather confused account of what they think. And you [the therapist] listen with your background and you don't know what they are saying, but you better know that you don't know. And then you need to try to do something that induces a change in the patient . . . any little change, because that patient wants a change, however small, and he will accept that as a change. He won't stop to measure the extent of that change. He will accept that as a change and then he will follow that change and the change will develop in accord with his own needs. . . . It's much like rolling a snowball down a mountainside. It starts out a small snowball, but as it rolls down it gets larger and larger . . . and it becomes an avalanche that fits the shape of the mountain.

— Milton Erickson, quoted in Gordan & Meyers-Anderson, 1981, pp. 16–17

problem, 1: a question posed for solution or consideration. **2:** a question, matter, situation, or person that is perplexing or difficult. **3:** in mathematics, anything required to be done, or requiring the doing of something. The *Thesaurus* lists these words: confusion, conundrum, difficul-

---

[1]The strikethrough is used here again to indicate that the term is being used without really being meant.

ty, dilemma, enigma, mystery, puzzle, quandary, riddle,
predicament, snag.

In the clinical context, we can read "problem" in a variety of
ways based on the dictionary and the thesaurus. One option is
to see the problems clients bring into therapy as fitting best
within the final part of the dictionary entry and Erickson's
injunction: anything that requires the doing of something.
More particularly, a problem is a puzzle, a riddle, or a predicament that requires the doing of something.

As suggested in previous chapters it can be useful in doing
therapy and/or talking about doing therapy to apply the philosophy of language to this particular use of language. Following
Jacques Derrida (1981), any concept — even, and particularly,
family resemblance type concepts — already carries the seed of
its deconstruction.

For instance, at the start of the session (described in Chapter
6) the problem "nymphomania" had the following criteria:

1. It was a compulsion.
2. It involved pathological sex, a problem deeply rooted in the
   woman's infancy.
3. It involved having sex for all the wrong reasons.
4. It was an indicator of a "bad marriage."
5. It served as a "sleeping pill."

This problem was deconstructed by inverting the fifth criterion
into the primary focus of a language game that lead the client
toward achieving the goal. She was able to sleep, to have sex for
the right reasons, and to see herself as involved in a good marriage.

It is not necessary to assume, for instance, that all problems
with the label "compulsion" are alike and/or that they are somehow distinctly different from other problems with other labels.
In fact, post-structualists might assume that problems are
more similar to each other than they are different. That is,
"phobias," "compulsions," "depressions," and "sexual problems,"
etc., can be seen as language games involving descriptions of
similar processes of problem formation, problem naming, prob-

lem maintenance, and, in the therapy situation, as language games involving the construction of a complaint from a problem, problem resolution, and solution development.

In some ways client problems are, however, more different than similar when we take a "person in his context" approach to describing the situation, rather than a formal "problem" approach. That is, any two "phobia" cases or two "depression" cases will differ widely when it comes to the language games involving the client's description of his life circumstances, family history, problem onset, failed solution attempts, goals for therapy, etc.

* * *

The whole concept of *problem/complaint* can be read to imply another concept, *nonproblem/noncomplaint* (i.e., exceptions,[2] times when the complaint/problem does not happen even though the client has reason to expect it to happen)[3] and, of course, the space between problem and nonproblem or the areas of life where the problem/nonproblem is not an issue and is not of concern to the client. This space between problem/nonproblem is also available to the client and therapist for use in constructing a solution.

> **exception,** anything deviating from the usual pattern or course. The *Thesaurus* lists: left out, ignored, excluded.

"'Exceptions' are those behaviors, perceptions, thoughts, and feelings that contrast with the complaint and have the

---

[2]White (1988) states that what he calls "unique outcomes" is the same as what we call "exceptions" (de Shazer, 1985, 1988; de Shazer et al., 1986) and states that the terms are "interchangeable" (p. 8). However, the word "unique" suggests that it is a one-time event and misses the point: Exceptions are times (rather, depictions of times) when the complaint is absent; the term "exceptions" always has a plural form.

Exceptions to the rule of the complaint are always seen as repeatable to the point where "the exception becomes the (new) rule," an idea missed entirely by the term "unique outcome" which implies nonrepeatability.

[3]Clients describe exceptions and/or pretherapy changes in at least two-thirds of cases (Weiner-Davis, de Shazer, & Gingerich, 1987).

potential of leading to a solution if amplified by the therapist and/or increased by the client" (Lipchik, 1988, p. 4). The concept of problem/complaint is *always* exposed to the possibility of accidents and/or exceptions. Like most concepts, it is binary, it has both an "inside" and an "outside." Although the concept's "inside" and its "outside" are distinct, the marker between "inside" and "outside" is not an impermeable barrier that marks "off the conceptual purity of X [inside] from everything that is not-X [outside]" (Staten, 1984, p. 18). Is this "outside" then a necessary, rather than a chance possibility; and if it is always and necessarily possible, is the concept of exception not then an *essential* possibility and an essential aspect of the concept of ~~problem~~, thus making the concept *undecidable*? The *undecidability* of the concept of problem/complaint, and other binary or oppositional concepts, is not a matter of simple ambiguity. Rather, this term, *undecidable* or *indecidable*, refers to concepts "that can no longer be included within binary opposition, but which, however, inhabit philosophical opposition, resisting and disorganizing it, *without ever* constituting a third term, without ever leaving room for a solution in the form of speculative dialectics" (Derrida, 1981, p. 43). Binary or oppositional concepts are undecidable because they suspend the apparent decidable opposition between what is "inside" and "outside." The "inside" and the "outside" are *necessarily* open to each other, contaminated by each other. But, without this "inside"/"outside" distinction, there would be no meaning and there would be no difference. Through this difference, meaning is constructed through use in interaction and in language games, and difference opens "out onto some possibilities that have not been conceivable under the old formulas" (Staten, 1984, p. 24).

CASE EXAMPLE TWO: A 50% IMPROVEMENT

A young man came to therapy because he wanted to solve his problem of exposing himself. As the therapist[4]

[4]Steve de Shazer

and the client talked about this, it became clear that the client saw his behavior as compulsive; he felt driven by his frequent urges (up to five urges in a day). However, over the previous three months, the client had made a 50% improvement. That is, before the start of therapy he was already overcoming half of his urges.

As client and therapist talk about the complaint (a language game that justifies or gives a rationale for therapy), in this case, the compulsion to expose himself, *any* mention of his not exposing himself when exposing himself is expected (since he had the urge) makes the concept of compulsion (a criteria of this ~~problem~~) into an *undecidable*. This begins the process of deconstructing the ~~problem~~ (and the concept of the ~~problem~~). Of course an *undecidable* already initiates the language game of solution construction (conversations that lead the client toward achieving the goal), because the exception – not exposing himself – is a criterion of the solution (a language game that specifies how to end therapy) and of the concept of solution, and not a criterion of the ~~problem~~.

The therapist then focused the conversation on these exceptions, those times when the client overcame the urge to expose himself. Under what conditions did the client overcome the urge? Under what conditions was the client more likely than not to overcome the urge? Under what conditions was the client least likely to overcome the urge? The client was able to describe what he did when he overcame the urge, but none of his strategies worked all the time.

Focusing on these exceptions rather than on the ~~problem~~ inverts the presumed hierarchy, making what is seemingly secondary into what is primary. That is, in this therapeutic conversation, times when he overcomes the urge are more important to constructing a solution than the times when he does not overcome the urge. This seems to violate common sense and the traditional structuralist position that there is something at the root of the ~~problem~~, something hidden that needs to be uncovered and worked on in order to solve the ~~problem~~.

As the conversation continued to focus on overcoming the urges, the client described his efforts at overcoming the urge to drink to excess (he had not done so in five months) and his continuing efforts to overcome his urge to use/abuse drugs. Again, most of his strategies were effective much of the time, but none was effective at overcoming all the urges. He saw his urge to drink as another compulsion and yet he had found a way to abstain for three whole months during the previous year.

Even though the client was able to richly describe his behaviors that were associated with the exceptions – overcoming the urges to (a) expose himself, (b) drink to excess, and (c) use drugs – he had very little confidence that his approach could actually lead to a "real" solution. Even though the client was able to describe these exceptions – times when the complaint is unexpectedly absent – as happening 50% of the time, he still perceived the ~~problem~~ pattern as the *dominant* one. After all, the steps that he had taken seemed very small in the face of his view of the problems as compulsive behaviors, overwhelming and beyond control.

Randomness, Spontaneity, Chance

The client described the exceptions as occurring randomly and therefore saw them as flukes or chance events. Regardless of which strategy he used, overcoming the urge was beyond his control. Thus, every time the complaint did not happen, it came as a surprise to him, and the exceptions – no matter how frequent they became and no matter how easy the behaviors involved were for him to do – were not perceived as models upon which to build a solution.

By describing exceptions as unimportant and beyond his purview, he failed to read them as evidence that his life was getting better and that he was more and more frequently over-

coming his compulsive urges. However much his description
implies control, it is difficult to prescribe these random or
chance conditions surrounding the exceptions as a means of
solution because he knows that they do not always work. It is
even more difficult for the client to have any confidence in his
ability to repeat the exceptions, no matter how frequent they
have been. All he can do is repeat the strategy and hope, with
little confidence that it will work at any particular time. This is
the problem of randomness. Wittgenstein (1975a) summarizes
it in the following way:

> If I now assume there could be a random series, then that is a
> series about which, by its very nature, nothing can be known
> apart from the fact that I can't know it. Or better, that it can't
> be known. (# 145).

At the end of the first and second sessions the client
was given a homework task asking him to predict the
night before whether or not he would overcome the urge to
expose himself the next day. Then he was to see when his
prediction turned out to be correct and to try to account
for how come he was either right or wrong in his prediction. In the second session, he reported that, although he
discovered that his predictions were not valid, nonetheless he overcame more of the urges than he had in the
weeks before the first session. He did learn that on days
when he was busy enough, he found ways to overcome
urges; when not busy enough, overcoming the urge was
less frequent.

Predicting Randomness, Spontaneity and Chance

Success at overcoming the urge to expose himself was *unpredictable*. However, the meaning or concept of the complaint can
become undecidable when the client is asked to predict the
exception, because this means that the therapist is suggesting
that the exception *is* predictable. When the presence of the

exception is seen as predictable, then the presence of the complaint is, at least implicitly, seen as unpredictable.

It is reasonable that before therapy begins the client would predict that the ~~problem~~ is going to happen rather than the exception, because the exception is seen as beyond control. However, there is no reason for the therapist to assume that exceptions are any more subject to chance than any other behavior, whether problematic or exceptional. Rather, it seems best to assume that these "random" exceptions are not random and are indeed embedded in certain, as yet undescribed, contexts or patterns which, if described, would allow for their being predicted and thus prescribed.

It seems clear that both the client and the therapist could safely predict continuation of the problematic behavior. It also seems safe to assume that the hit-or-miss occurrence of random exceptions could be predicted, even though any specific occurrence of the exceptions appears beyond prediction.

All this seems common sense: "Random" exceptions are not really random, they are just described as if they were because the conditions which would allow us to predict them are unknown. What does not seem common sense is that predicting exceptions tends to increase the frequency of the exceptions. For instance, asking a client "to each day predict whether you will overcome the urge to do coke the following day and then, at the end of the day see if your prediction turned out right, and then, account for how come your prediction turned out right or wrong" most frequently will lead to a reported increase in the client's overcoming the urge to do coke, even though the pattern involved remains undescribed.

The task of predicting random exceptions is designed to create a self-fulfilling prophecy. That is, predicting an atypical situation (e.g., the client overcoming the urge to expose himself) can lead to behaviors that increase the likelihood of the exception, which changes the typical situation (exposing himself) into an atypical one. It is as if the client knew all along what the elements of the exception pattern were, but was simply unable to describe them. It is as if the prediction of the exception triggers the exception pattern itself, even when the client remains unable to describe this pattern in subsequent sessions. It might be best to see predicting exceptions as if it involved the whole pattern surrounding the exceptions, even when the pattern remains unknown.

In the third session,[5] he reported that on 14 of the 27 days between sessions he had been urge-free and that he had overcome all his urges during the interval except one. But he could not explain the absence of the urge except to point to having a job that kept him busy. As a task, he was asked to predict, each night, whether the next day would be an urge-free day. Urge-free days continued to predominate until, several months later, he reported that he had been completely urge-free for two months, was no longer drinking, was no longer taking drugs, and had a job. Six months later, in addition to these changes, he was going to college and had a girl friend.

The meaning of the concept of "exhibitionism," a male sexual dysfunction, is divided off and separated from "non-exhibition-ism." Part of the meaning "exhibitionism" held for the young man was that "flashing" was the result of a driving, overwhelming compulsion that included uncontrollable urges, a desire for closeness and intimacy, and importantly, an escape from boredom. However, even at the start of therapy, the border between the two was not firm: 50% of the time he overcame the urge. In this case, one of the criteria (uncontrollable urge) was undermined before the inversion of criteria and the problem/concept. The solution-focused language game brought these exceptions into the primary position and broadened the field by including what had been excluded. The conversations during the sessions and the interventions were designed, for pragmatic and therapeutic purposes, to begin to exclude the exhibitionism and to stabilize the meaning of his situation around the overcoming and eventual elimination of the urges.

[5]See Chapter 10 for more on this case.

CASE EXAMPLE THREE: FIVE DAYS AGO ...

The husband began by talking about the problems in the marriage, all of which he blamed on himself. As he saw it, he was depressed and, every once in a while he would get very angry at his wife due to his deep-seated anger. He did not think that either of them wanted to divorce, but at times he thought that she was ready to end it. From her point of view, they did not communicate. This meant that when she talked, he ran away; when she confronted him, he ran away. Whenever she looked for him, he was working, either on his job or around the house.

Therapist[6]: When was the most recent time when things were OK or better than OK?

Husband: The past five or six days . . .

Wife: . . . immediately after I called setting this up.

T: Really? What's been different?

H: I've felt some hope about things, and we talked and I guess that we renewed our commitment.

W: We've been, ah, . . . courteous, and haven't argued.

T: How would a movie of these five days be different from a movie of the five days before that?

In fact, they had sex for the first time in months, the family ate together, there was more affection in general. He had spontaneously come home during a break at work, and they had joined together in an argument with his mother, rather than letting his mother get them arguing.

Although exceptions are frequently read as related to the clients' complaints, they can also be read as precursors to goals (language games that lead the client toward setting and achieving goals), and solutions (a language game that marks the termination of therapy). That is, times when the complaints are

---

[6]Steve de Shazer

unexpectedly absent can be seen as (a) times when the goal-state is approximated and/or (b) the raw material for constructing the solution. The couple wanted to get along – he wanted to feel better, to be less angry, and she wanted to nag less.

It was clear to both of them that these five-days were quite "good enough." If most five-day periods over the course of the subsequent six months were like these five exceptional days, they would be more than satisfied. Furthermore, they were 80% confident that they could do it deliberately for the next two weeks and that, in six months' time, they would be able to report having had the majority of days feel like these past five days.

In this case, the telephone call began the therapy: The ~~problem~~ was already being deconstructed and the solution well underway. This presession change is thus focused upon and relocated into a primary position and the behaviors associated spontaneously with the telephone call, the nonproblematic five days, are used to begin a language game constructing a therapeutic solution.

*   *   *

The conversations that therapists and clients have can be seen as stories, as narratives. Like any story, each case or each session of each case has a beginning, a middle, and an ending, or at least a sense of an ending. Like any story, the conversation is held together by the patterns involved, by the plot. Like many stories, therapy conversations deal with human predicaments, troubles, resolutions, and attempted resolutions.

Viewed as stories, the conversations between therapists and clients are subject to change within and across situations as they negotiate and deal with the issues emergent in their conversations. Indeed, the discontinuities and transformations in meaning may be understood as changes in therapists' and clients' storytelling activities. Such changes partly involve the development of new "plots," like the inversion of the ~~problem~~ and exception themes. That is, new depictions of events are linked together to produce new patterns and meanings. It is through their depictions of unexpected events and exceptions as aspects of larger patterns of solution development that therapists and clients construct clients' lives. Further, in developing new plots, therapists and clients recast the predicaments of clients' lives and their attempts to manage them.

One of the advantages of conceptualizing therapy conversations as story construction and telling is that it allows us to compare and evaluate the narrative structures of different types of therapy conversations.

According to Gergen and Gergen (1983, 1986), story construction is an activity focused partly on such questions as "Is she a good or bad person?" "Is he getting better or worse?" and "Am I really achieving what I want?" Such questions require that people describe their lives and those of others across time. They must link otherwise discrete events into patterns that can be used to produce and justify their conclusions that the issues at hand are better, worse or the same. Thus, Gergen and Gergen conclude that there are three narrative types available to people in describing and evaluating their own and other people's lives. There are:

1. *Progressive* narratives that justify the conclusion that people and situations are progressing toward their goals,
2. *Stability* narratives that justify the conclusion that life is unchanging, and
3. *Digressive* narratives[7] that justify the conclusion that life is moving away from their goals.

Specifically, we may ask, are some types of story construction more likely to result in change or solution talk than others? Specifically, solution-determined narratives are more likely than complaint-centered narratives (the major form of therapeutic story construction) to produce transformations and discontinuities.

---

[7]Gergen and Gergen (1983, 1986) use the term "regressive," but "digressive" better emphasizes the movement away from the goal.

Analysis of therapeutic conversations as progessive, stability, and digressive narratives is useful for assessing whether desired change is occurring. Clearly, stability narratives are problematic for therapists and clients because they signal and are sources for perceived lack of change in clients' problems and lives. Although both progressive and digressive narratives involve some sort of change, they have very different implications for therapy conversations.

Progressive narratives are sources for producing desired changes, whereas digressive narratives involve undesired changes. Indeed, as Gergen and Gergen note, digressive or regressive narrative structure is central to the telling of tragic stories which focus on people's movement away from their desired life circumstances.

Therapists' concerns and responsibilities in therapy conversations also vary depending on the types of narratives or stories that dominate in their interactions with clients. Their major concern and responsibility in conversations dominated by stability and digressive narratives is to help clients construct new stories that signal and are sources for desired change. The development of such stories involves transformations in therapists' and clients' conversation.

Therapists' major concern and responsibility in therapy conversations dominated by progressive narratives are to help clients elaborate on and "confirm" their stories, expanding and developing exception and change themes into solution themes (Gingerich et al., 1988). Therapists may do so by pointing to ways in which clients are attaining their goals and helping them develop new and related goals that involve further change in their lives. Therapeutic narratives focused on the setting and attainment of workable goals are more effective in producing change than those focused on clients' complaints.

SYSTEM AGAIN

These stories and narratives take on the attributes of a system. That is, it is the whole of the story, or at least the whole of a narrative told jointly by the client and the therapist in a session, that is different from the sum of its parts, which include both the client's depiction of the situation and the therapist's description from a different perspective. This is the most readily available interactional behavior.

9

THERAPEUTIC CHANGE
Case Examples Two (Again) and Four

When therapists use the word/concept "change," what do they mean? Conceptually, the most common use in the family therapy discourse is change in the system, systemic change, structural change, etc. For instance, Hoffman (1981) and Simon et al. (1985) follow Watzlawick et al. (1974) in drawing a distinction between first-order change and second-order change.

> change, a system is able to change in two ways: 1: Individual parameters change in a continuous manner but the structure of the system does not alter; this is known as "first-order change." 2: The system changes qualitatively and in a discontinuous manner; this is known as "second-order change". This second type of change in systems occurs with "changes in the body of rules governing their structure or internal order" (Watzlawick et al., 1974, p. 11). Second-order change is change of change. (Simon et al., 1985, p. 33)

They draw a distinction between (a) continuous change, changes that are observed to happen in a step-by-step fashion, and (b) discontinuous change, changes that are observed to happen by leaps. Furthermore, Watzlawick et al. (1974), Hoffman (1981), and Simon et al. (1985) attribute second-order change to so-called "paradoxical interventions," involving a muddle of a different sort.

Second-order or discontinuous change is sometimes also confusingly called "morphogenesis" (Simon et al., 1985) following Maruyama (1963), who described changes in systems this way:

> [Once a system] is kicked in a right direction and with sufficient initial push, the deviation-amplifying mutual positive feedbacks take over the process, and the resulting development will be disproportionally large as compared with the initial kick. (p. 166)

However, "deviation-amplification is *not necessarily* discontinuous" and in fact "most of the time it is not" (Maruyama, 1981). Also, Thom's "Catastrophe Theory" (1975) points out that continuous causes may lead to discontinuous effects. Sometimes Hoffman (1981) and Simon et al. (1985) use the term systemic "transformation" when talking about change. Other words/concepts concerning change are also used, such as symptomatic change, individual change, structural change, psychodynamic change, insight, and behavioral change. (Does insight come first, before behavioral change? Can behavioral change come first and insight follow? Is just behavioral change enough?) Whatever these distinctions might mean, do they matter to the client or to the therapist?

Therapists use any or all of these words to point to what they want to see happen in therapy. Therapists want their clients to show them (in some way) a change, to point to a difference (an unrecognized difference does not make a difference), to point to something that is not the same damn thing over and over. They want clients to show some modification of their thoughts, feelings, attitudes, perceptions, and/or behaviors; to point to having substituted something "positive" for something "negative." In short, therapists want clients to depict their life outside of the therapy situation as being, in some way significantly different at the end of therapy from what it was at the start.

When we look at a therapy session, what will we see that shows change? How does the client depict change? What will we see that shows the client and therapist doing something that brings about or sets the conditions for therapeutic change? How is change promoted in the therapeutic conversation?

* * *

In 1981 I developed an interactional constructivist theory of therapeutic change, metaphorically named "a binocular theory of change" (de Shazer, 1982a), or better, when dealing either with a team and/or with a couple or family unit, "a polyocular (Maruyama, 1977) theory of change." This name is used to take advantage of the way depth perception develops as a metaphor for the way therapeutic change seems to develop.

Depth perception is a bonus derived from the fact that what the right eye sees is somewhat different from what the left eye sees. Neither eye alone is able to perceive the depth that the two eyes together perceive. If the eyes are too far apart or too close together there is no depth perception.

In the clinical context, clients describe their situation from their own particular, unique point of view. The therapist listens, always seeing things differently, and redescribes what the client describes from a different point of view. A bonus accrues when the two slightly different descriptions (binocularity) are put together. The result is not the client's view and it is not the therapist's view, but something different from both. But, as with the two eyes, if the descriptions are too far apart or too similar, this bonus is lost. When the therapist is part of a team and the other members are behind the see-through mirror, then more redescriptions (polyocularity) of what the client describes are developed and the chances of developing a fit are increased, and/or the process is made easier or is potentially accelerated. But the team is not necessary for therapy to be seen as an interactional constructivist endeavor.

One needs only a therapist and a client for two descriptions to develop, as long as the two descriptions are clearly similar yet also different enough. For example, if the client says that he is depressed and therefore he does not play golf, this can be juxtaposed with the therapist's view that the client does not play golf and therefore he is depressed. In a family situation where the parents think that their son is smart but acting dumb, the therapist might wonder if the boy is dumb but— being a gifted actor—has fooled everybody into thinking he is smart. In either case, enough detail might be added to the therapist's description so that the client can see the similarity of what is being described, begin to describe things differently himself, and thus behave differently. He might force himself to play golf to see if he felt better afterward. Or the parents might quit nagging the kid about homework (since too much had been expected from the boy), which might lead the kid to actually do his homework (to prove that he is not so dumb after all).

This different view developed by the therapist, who necessarily already sees things differently, is given more substance when clients describe exceptions or criteria that support the therapist's redescription: times when he played golf even though he felt depressed and ended up feeling better, or times when the parents did not nag and the boy did his homework. In these situations, the therapist's different view will fit more readily because the clients have already had the experience, even though they dismissed it as a fluke, as something trivial in the face of what they perceive as the all encompassing nature of the deeply rooted problem.

* * *

Foucault's (1972) three categories of transformation might be a useful framework for thinking about and describing how depictions of change are developed and promoted in the therapeutic context. Progressive narratives often include these characteristic types of depiction:

1. *Derivations*, changes developed by passing to the complementary or alternate meaning of a term, e.g., (a) problem/complaint—exceptions, (b) predictability—unpredictability, (c) uncontrolled—controlled, (d) happen—do;

2. *mutations*, changes by displacing boundaries defining the field, e.g., (a) bringing in depictions of absent parties, (b) pursuing depictions of what is "better" when the client is depicting nonchange, (c) inviting more or fewer people to the next session; and
3. *redistributions*, changes by reversal in hierarchical order, e.g., inverting what was secondary into a primary position.

In Foucault's historical and archaeological view, any "change occurs through chance, which appears to us as discontinuous transformation" (Leitch, 1983, p. 149), which certainly fits with the depictions of change offered by most clients.

* * *

The following two verbatim quotations of sections from therapy sessions illustrate the kinds of things therapists point to when they use the word/concept "change."

CASE EXAMPLE TWO (AGAIN): A 50% IMPROVEMENT[1]

The Episode of the Lost Urge
At the start of the third session,
[Unit 1] Therapist[2]: So, what's different with you?
[2] Client: Ummm. Well, I got a job [after many months of being unemployed] that keeps me real busy.
[3] T: Good.
[4] C: In fact, for, since I last saw you [this third session was 25 days after the second], I've been kind of losing interest in exposing myself.
[5] T: How did you do that?

The therapist is trying to shift the depiction of the loss of the urge from one involving something spontaneous, something that just happened, to a depiction involving something that the client did.

---

[1]See Chapter 8 for more on this case.
[2]Steve de Shazer

[6] C: For a while, I completely lost interest in exposing myself.

[7] T: How did you do that?

[8] C: I just wasn't interested. I just don't have the urge anymore.

[9] T: How did you do that?

[10] C: It almost came natural to me. The more I paid attention to the job, the less I paid attention to the urge.

[11] T: Good.

[12] C: The last time I had the urge was two days ago. Before that . .

[13] T: (*Interrupting*) Did you overcome that urge?[3]

[14] C: Yeah. But before that, before that it was a week since I had the urge.

At the start of therapy, one month earlier, he saw himself as a helpless exhibitionist, as driven by a compulsion to expose himself. Now, he says, the urge is getting lost and this is coming naturally to him. This is the kind of conversation, the kind of client depictions, that therapists point to in order to illustrate what they mean by "change."

CASE EXAMPLE FOUR: A LONG MIRACLE

In the first session, after the couple had described the "troubles" of the previous six months that brought them to therapy, the therapist[4] asked

[Unit 71]: When was the most recent time when things were "normal"?

[72] Mrs. J: Since we called three weeks ago, we've been getting along great. We're talking through things.

---

[3]In the previous session, the client had been asked to "observe what you do when you overcome the urge to expose yourself."

[4]Steve de Shazer

[73] Mr. J: Yeah.

[74] T: Back to the way things were six months ago before the "troubles" started?

[75] Mrs. J: To a great extent.

[76] Mr. J: Or better.

[77] T: How come? What are you doing?

[78] Mrs. J: I'm accepting him more lately; more patient than I've been.

[79] T: What do you do that's "more accepting"?

[80] Mrs. J: Sometimes he's tougher on my son than I am and I'm trying to not be so judgmental. Maybe that's just his style: We can parent differently.

. . .

[91] T: What have you noticed different in the past three weeks?

[92] Mr. J: I've felt more relaxed and it just seems that there is not quite as much asked of me as far as parenting goes. Things have calmed down. We've gotten a babysitter a few times.

[93] T: That's different?

[94] Mr. J: Yeah, it's a first. I've tried to accept her parenting style too and to not think that she's spoiling him all the time.

. . .

[120] T: If the boy were here, and I was to ask him what he's noticed different about you two in the past three weeks, what would he say?

[121] Mr. J: He'd say that we've not fought as much.

[122] T: What else?

[123] Mr. J: I haven't got as upset with him and not as often as I did in the past.

[124] Mrs. J: He'd notice that you're in a better mood and that I've been home more.

. . .

[130] T: What difference have you noticed in the boy?

[131] Mrs. J: He's willing to stay home by himself.

[132] T: That's new?

[133] Mrs. J: Yeah. And generally more independent in the past couple of weeks. He's more relaxed too.

[134] T: Anything else?

[135] Mr. J: He's been in a pretty good mood and more cooperative about chores.

[136] T: You've told me a lot about what was different about these past three weeks and, this may sound stupid but, if, six months from now, things were about like they've been these three weeks, would that be at least minimally OK for the two of you? The three of you?

[137] Mr. J: I think so.

[138] Mrs. J: Yeah, for all three.

[139] T: So, the thing is, how do you keep it going at least? Or even better?

The clients said, throughout the session, that these changes spontaneously developed immediately after they set up this appointment. Even though this is a good example of pretreatment changes, it is nonetheless exactly the kind of conversation that therapists point to when they use the word/concept "change." Units 120 through 124 and 130 through 135 are depictions of so-called "systemic change," or at least what therapists point to when illustrating "systemic change." Clearly, units 136 through 138 show that the changes they are depicting are satisfactory for them.

Interestingly and importantly, the first "therapeutic intervention" was their phone call setting up the appointment and the second was asking about and exploring exceptions, times when the problem/complaint was unexpectedly absent.

To be truly satisfying, it seems that the presession changes need to be certified by the therapist as worthwhile changes, to be marked as authentic and real. Without these markers, it seems that the changes cannot be experienced as authentic and real—thus the couple is unsure enough of these changes to come to therapy even though the solution process is well underway.

Does this interactional constructivist process of signification, of helping the client to construct what the client did differently into a difference that makes a difference, imply that the social signification is more important than the behavioral and perceptual changes themselves? Do the clients need therapy to remind them of what they did, to make what they did worthwhile? Is this what therapy does for clients?

* * *

Conceptual debates about first-order change and second-order change and about continuous or discontinuous change seem irrelevant within the context of therapeutic conversations. Change is change as long as it is satisfactory to clients, as long as the changes they depict are ones that indicate to them that a solution has developed.

Change is a constant, never-ending process. Nothing ever remains the same, nothing ever repeats. No matter how much something appears to happen over and over, no matter how redundant it appears or how much it seems to be the same damn thing over and over again, nonetheless each iteration is at least subtly different. Minimally, each so-called repetition has all of the previous times as part of its historical context and meaning. Furthermore, each so-called repetition also has all of its predicted recurrences as another significant part of its context and meaning.

As we have seen (case example one), by a reversal in hierarchical order – a *redistribution* in Foucault's terms – a woman's concept of nymphomania can be inverted, made undecidable, and solved as insomnia. A different point of view was brought to bear on the couple's situation (case example four), when the therapist asked about exceptions, attempting to develop a *derivation* – to pass over to the alternative. Once they depicted "system wide" exceptions (change through *mutation*), the clinical task was no longer to end the ~~problem/complaint~~ but rather to increase the already present exceptions.

10

WHAT DOES THE SOLUTION SOLVE?
Case Examples Five and Six

> *A Japanese coastal village was once threatened by a tidal wave,*
> *but the wave was sighted in advance, far out on the horizon, by a*
> *lone farmer in the rice fields on the hillside above the village. At*
> *once he set fire to the fields, and the villagers who came swarm-*
> *ing up to save their crops were saved from flood.*

> *—Japanese folktale*

Frequently, the relationship between the ~~problem~~ and the solution in therapy is similar to the relationship between the problem and the solution in this Japanese folktale. The problem here is that the villagers were threatened by the tidal wave, but the farmer who saw the danger was too far away to yell or run to the village to alert everybody. So he ruled out the impossible, which in this case would appear to leave no alternative way to help the villagers save themselves. The problem situation looked unsolvable.

Knowing the dependence of the villagers on their rice crop, the farmer was able to do something different, something outside the conditions or parameters of the problem (i.e., a *mutation*): He did not circumscribe his thinking as needing to be within the "tidal wave-villagers-too distant farmer" set. His goal was to save the villagers and so he set a new problem, created a new task that solved the original "tidal wave problem" more or less by accident. The villagers were not saving themselves from the tidal wave; they were saving their rice crop. Importantly, for the sake of therapists and clients alike, the "fire problem" bears no relationship whatsoever to the original problem description, and yet the original problem was solved!

This folktale is a provocative and suggestive prototype that we can see as clearly related to the various case examples used so far. The nymphomania was solved by setting a new task of solving the insomnia problem. The exhibitionism problem was solved by setting up the task of finding ways to increase the frequency of the exceptions, which, by accident, led to his losing the urge to expose himself.

A BONUS CASE EXAMPLE

Milton H. Erickson (in Haley, 1967b) reports on a case:

> This case history centers around an impasse reached during therapy and the utilization of a fantasy about the future to secure an effective resumption of therapeutic progress.
>
> The patient suffered from a profound anxiety neurosis with severe depressive and withdrawal reactions and marked dependency patterns. A great deal of hypnotherapy had been done and her early response was good. However, as therapy continued, she became increasingly negative and resistive.
>
> Finally, the situation became one in which she limited herself, during the therapeutic hour, to an intellectual appraisal of her problems and her needs, while rigidly maintaining the *status quo* at all other times.
>
> A few examples will suffice to illustrate her behavior. She could not, for cogent reasons, tolerate her parental home situation but she persisted in remaining in it despite actual difficulties and in the face of favorable opportunities to leave. She resented her employment situation bitterly, but refused to accept a promotion actually available. She recognized fully her need for social activities but avoided, often with difficulty, all opportunities. She discussed at length her interest in reading and the long hours she spent in her room futilely wishing for something to read, but she refused to enter the library she passed twice daily, despite numerous promises to herself.

Additionally, she became increasingly demanding that the writer must, perforce, take definitive action to compel her to do those things she recognized as necessary and proper but which she could not bring herself to do.

After many futile hours, she finally centered her wishful thinking upon the idea that, if she could achieve even one of the desired things, she would then have the impetus and firmness of intention to achieve the others.

After she had emphasized and reemphasized this statement, it was accepted at face value.

She was then immediately hypnotized deeply, and, in the somnambulistic state, instructed to see a whole series of crystal balls. In each of these would be depicted a significant experience in her life. These she was to study, making comparisons, drawing contrasts, and noting the continuity of various elements from one age level to another. Out of this study would slowly emerge a constellation of ideas which would be formulated without her awareness. This formulation would become manifest to her through another and larger crystal ball in which she would see herself depicted *pleasantly, happily and desirably, in some future activity*.

She spent approximately an hour absorbedly studying the various hallucinatory scenes, now and then glancing about the office as if looking for the other crystal ball.

Finally, she located it and thereupon gave all of her attention to it, describing the hallucinated scene to the writer with interest.

It was the depiction of a wedding scene of a lifelong family friend which, in actuality, was not to take place for more than three months. (pp. 379–380) [Emphasis added]

Between this session and the wedding, Erickson saw her twice because she wanted "to remember in her unconscious very clearly all that she had seen and thought and felt as she watched the wedding scene" (p. 380). She then terminated therapy.

After the real wedding, her explanation was that she, Nadine and the bridegroom had been lifelong friends and that their families were intimate friends. Some months ago, following a

therapeutic session, she had felt impelled to discontinue therapy and to devote her energies to getting ready for that wedding.
When she was asked to be a bridesmaid, she decided to make
her own dress. This had made it necessary to get promoted at
work so that she would have better hours. Then she had taken
an apartment in town so that she would not lose a total of three
hours going back and forth from work. She had gone on shopping tours with various friends to help select wedding presents
and she had arranged "showers" for the bride-to-be. All in all,
she had been exceedingly and happily busy. . . .

Finally she was reminded of her original purpose in seeing
the writer. Her reply was simply, "I was a pretty sick girl when I
first came to see you. I was horribly mixed up and I'm grateful
to you for getting me straightened out in time so that I could
get ready for the wedding." She had no awareness that her preparations for the wedding constituted her recovery. (p. 381)

Is this magic? Remember that, according to Erickson, "the
patient suffered from a profound anxiety neurosis with severe
depressive and withdrawal reactions and marked dependency
patterns" (p. 379). How does her imagining a highly specific
future event, one that involves a vision of the solved problem,
work to cure what Erickson himself in 1954[1] called "a profound
anxiety neurosis," etc.?

Writing a case history is a form of storytelling, and Erickson
is a prime example of the storyteller. His case examples often
read like short stories, with or without a teaching or illustrative
purpose. This is part of the fascination Erickson holds for therapists.

Erickson's storytelling illustrates how he linked events and
gave them meaning. Case studies, like other stories, have be-
ginnings, middles, and endings that are held together by the
patterns of the events (which might be called plots as they are
in fiction). Assuming that Erickson meant what he said when
he started this story with a diagnosis, that the patient had a
deep psychic or mental disorder with a partially disorganized

[1] 1954 was the publication date of the original article, "Pseudo-Orientation in
Time as a Hypnotherapeutic Procedure."

personality, *and* that he meant what he said when he wrote that "she had no awareness that her preparations for the wedding constituted her recovery," how are we to read this story? What can this story possibly mean about Erickson's views of clients' or patients' problems and his view of neurosis, keeping in mind the professional meanings attached to the term in the early 1950s when this paper was written? What can this mean about Erickson's view of therapy? The words used in the middle and ending cause us to wonder and have doubts about the words used at the beginning of the story, where Erickson situates his case within a certain traditional, psychodynamic, and psychiatric context. As a master storyteller, he leads us to expect one particular kind of story; he sets us up to expect a certain kind of middle with a Freudian plot and a certain kind of ending. The surprise plot, with its untraditional middle and ending, make whatever Erickson might have meant by the diagnosis undecidable.

We are left with a simply told story about setting and achieving goals and about how focusing on accomplishing one specific, well defined task accidentally helps the young woman accomplish other tasks along the way. Once the goal – solving the wedding problem – was set, getting ready for the wedding allowed Erickson's patient to solve the problems that had brought her to therapy and get on with her new life.

GOALS, PRAGMATISM, PRAGMATICS

The use of "pragmatics" in family therapy is quite distinct from pragmatism "a system which tests the validity of all concepts by their practical results." The study of human communication (language and symbols) can be subdivided into three areas: (a) syntactics, the relationship of signs and symbols as in grammar; (b) semantics, the relationship of symbols and referents; and (c) pragmatics, the relationship of symbols and behavior. "While a clear conceptual separation is thus possible of the three areas, they are nevertheless interdependent" (Watzlawick et al., 1967, p. 22).

symbol, 1: something that stands for or represents another thing; especially, an object used to represent something abstract. **2**: a written or printed mark, letter, abbreviation, etc., standing for an object, quality, process, quantity. **3**: in psychoanalysis, an act or object representing an unconscious desire that has been repressed. *syn.* token, emblem, mark, badge, device, character, letter, writing

Thus, a symbol is that which stands for something else, something which represents something else, something that is perhaps "repressed." If "pragmatics" is one area of the study of human communication (language and behavior) and it is concerned with the connection between "symbols" and behavior, what could "pragmatics" mean? This definition suggests that language is symbolic, i.e., it suggests a structural perspective. But is not language (verbal and nonverbal) behavior? From a post-structural perspective, in language, these so-called symbols are just words, words like any other words. So, pragmatics is concerned with the relationship between words (as a special category of behavior) and other categories of behavior.

In the therapy situation, language (words, gestures, facial expressions, etc.) is the only behavior available for study. Although it may seem obvious and trivial, when the family comes into therapy with the parents complaining about the child's wetting the bed, all that happens in therapy is the depiction of these problematic events and not the events themselves. The client may *know* he is depressed, but all that happens in the therapy situation is that he depicts this depression, he describes feeling depressed. When he is talking with the therapist, he has to use criteria to define what he means by the word "depressed" and, therefore, what he is depicting is always open to therapeutic misunderstanding.

Therapeutic misunderstanding involves the development of a solution-focused language game out of a ~~problem/complaint~~ - focused one. As we have seen, this shift happens when the therapist focuses the conversation on those aspects of the client's depiction that contaminate or undermine the meaning of the client's complaint for the client and thus make whatever the client is depicting into something undecidable. What was seen as primary becomes secondary and what was secondary becomes primary; in other words, the exceptions become more important than the complaint and/or criteria become more important than what they were criteria for.

PRAGMATISM

Clients are seeking practical results when they come to therapy; they are pragmatists. They are "in pain," and they want to get rid of the ~~problem~~, plain and simple. But knowing that you have been successful at getting rid of something is difficult; the absence of something is hard to know.

Let's try to imagine the absence of being depressed, or better, the absence of feeling depressed. How do you do that? Is it like imagining the absence of the chair you are sitting in? Do you imagine sitting on the floor or a different chair? An empty space? Are you not comparing sitting on the floor with sitting in the chair that you are imagining is absent? The same things are involved in imagining the absence of feeling depressed: It always involves comparing the absence of feeling depressed with the presence of feeling nondepressed. This brings the depressed feeling into memory for sake of comparison. Does this lead, perhaps inevitably, to relapse?

Is it not far easier to imagine simply that you have purchased a new, leather chair and that this new chair is the one you are now sitting in while reading this? Does this not simply make the old chair absent in your imagination without your having to hold the old chair in your imagination for the sake of comparison?

The concept of "absent" implies the concept of "nonabsent" or "present." It is, of course, much easier to know that something different is present than it is to know that something is absent. This leads to the idea that the absence of the complaint implies the presence of a goal.

Goals are, according to Haley (1987), the "changes everyone, including the problem child, wants from therapy" (p. 38). They need to be clear and specific "so that a therapist can know when she has succeeded" (p. 39) and the client, too, can know success.

> **goal,** the end or final purpose; the end to which a design
> tends or which a person aims to reach or accomplish. The
> *Thesaurus* lists: object, end, aim, ambition.

According to Ackerman (1966):

> The ideal of family therapy is not merely to remove symptoms
> but to nourish a new way of life. Its goals are to remove emotion-
> al distress and disablement and promote the level of health and
> growth, both in the family group and its members by relieving
> pathogenic conflict and anxiety; by raising the level of comple-
> mentation [sic][2] of emotional needs; by strengthening the immu-
> nity of the family against critical upsets; by enhancing the har-
> mony and balance of family functions; by strengthening the
> individual member against destructive forces, both within him
> and surrounding him in the family environment; and by influ-
> encing the orientation of family identity and values toward
> health and growth. (p. 406)

For Minuchin et al. (1978), "The goal of therapy is to facili-
tate the growth of a system that encourages the freedom to
individuate while preserving the connectedness of belonging"
(p. 91), which is quite difficult to measure; therefore, "the therapeutic outcome was evaluated in two areas: a medical assessment of the degree of remission of anorexia symptoms and a
clinical assessment of psychosocial functioning in relation to
home, school, and peers." (p. 132).[3]

In the MRI brief therapy model, the therapist, in conjunction with the client, works out the definition of the therapeutic
goals. The therapist asks each client to describe in concrete
terms what his or her minimum goal for the therapy is, and to

---

[2]Perhaps Ackerman is here pointing to a tit-for-tat or complementary relationship between needs.

[3]"86% of the cases were recovered from both the anorexia and its psychosocial
components" (Minuchin et al., 1978, p. 133).

describe how each of them would recognize that this goal had been achieved (Weakland et al., 1974).

At BFTC, the therapist helps clients to describe their goals for therapy in concrete, specific terms. Various questions are used to help the clients describe how they will know when the problem is solved and to describe who will be doing what to whom, when, and where, after the problem is solved.

Without clear, concise ways to know whether it has either failed or succeeded, therapy can go on endlessly – which at times means that therapist and client succeed without their knowing it. Regardless of what else may result from it, a therapy conversation that is unending is a partial failure because one goal of therapy should be to resolve clients' complaints and terminate therapy as quickly as possible.

Early in their conversations, therapists and clients address the question, "How do we know when to stop meeting like this?" Both clinical experience and research indicate that workable goals[4] tend to have the following general characteristics. They are:

1. small rather than large;
2. salient to clients;
3. described in specific, concrete behavioral terms;
4. achievable within the practical contexts of clients' lives;
5. perceived by the clients as involving their "hard work";
6. described as the "start of something" and not as the "end of something";
7. treated as involving new behavior(s) rather than the absence or cessation of existing behavior(s).

Thus goals are depictions of what will be *present*, what will be happening in the clients' lives when the complaint is absent,

[4]Although the concepts of goal setting and achievement are often thought of as rather linear, we are using them in this construction as a way to promote change and elicit news of change and solution. Within our framework, multiple, interactional, and situational goal statements that describe the "who, what, when, where, and how" of solution are more desirable than single-targeted behavioral goal statements.

when the pain that brought them to therapy is absent and they therefore no longer depict life in problematic terms.

* * *

Suppose that one night there is a miracle and while you are sleeping the problem that brought you into therapy is solved: How would you know? What would be different? (de Shazer, 1988, p. 5)

What will you notice different the next morning that will tell you that there has been a miracle? What will your spouse notice?

The second part of this "miracle question" is a little more difficult than simply imagining that you have replaced your chair. Once the question becomes interactional, it is like being asked to imagine someone else's imagining what kind of new chair you purchased.

The framework of the miracle question and other questions of this type allows clients to bypass their structural, causal assumptions. They do not have to imagine the process of getting rid of the ~~problem~~, only the results. This then allows them to bring more of their previous nonproblem experiences into the conversation; thus, the goals developed from the miracle question are not limited to just getting rid of the ~~problem/complaint~~. Clients frequently are able to construct answers to this "miracle question" quite concretely and specifically. "Easy, I'll be able to say 'no' to cocaine." "She'll see me smile more and go to work with more enthusiasm."

CASE EXAMPLE FIVE: ONLY PRETENDING

In the first session, neither mother nor father was able to imagine the day after a miracle. They could not see their son changing even though they still had hopes of change. Their 15-year-old son, however, gave the following:

Son: I will get up at 7:30 without anybody calling me. I
    will take a shower and put the towel into the hamper,
    get dressed, go downstairs and eat breakfast—remem-
    bering to put my dirty dishes into the dishwasher.
    Then I will catch the first bus to school, get to school
    on time, and go to all my classes—and maybe even
    learn something. Then I will catch the first bus home,
    do my homework, set the table for supper, eat supper
    with the family, put the dirty dishes in the dishwash-
    er, and then go out with my friends, getting home by
    10:30.

Father: That would be a miracle!

The parents had situated their current problems as a continuation and development of a long line of problems. Over the
course of 10 years, there had been no time when there had not
been at least one of them in therapy concerning the son's problems. The son, who did not see the current situation in the
same way, was able to describe the goal in such a way that both
parents were able to say that, should what he described happen, then indeed the problem would be solved.

Since the son had described the day after the miracle in
such concrete and specific terms, the therapist[5] asked him
secretly to pick two days, one in each of the coming two
weeks, on which he would pretend and act as if the miracle
had happened, and to observe how his parents, his peers,
and the school personnel reacted. His parents were asked
simply to observe and to see if separately they could figure out which two days he picked.

Pretending or behaving as if the miracle has happened again
serves to disconnect the solution construction and development process from the problem/complaint and to bypass the
clients' historical, structural perspective and any disagreements about what the problem really is. Once the solution de-

---

[5] Insoo Kim Berg with Steve de Shazer behind the mirror.

velops, once clients know that the ~~problem~~ is solved, it no longer matters to them (or anyone else) what the ~~problem~~ might have been.

Two weeks later, dad said that the son had pretended on Tuesday of the first week and Wednesday of the second. Mother disagreed. She said it had been Thursday of the first week and Tuesday of the second. The son said they were both wrong: It had been Wednesday of the first week and Monday of the second.

Father: Regardless. It was the best two weeks in the entire history of our family.

In the course of seven sessions spread over the next six months, the parents' doubts about the solution, begun between sessions one and two, diminished. And additional, specific desired goals were met. As a closing task the parents were asked to:

T: Observe whatever signs there might be that will tell you whether he is still pretending or is just pretending to pretend.

Of course, things are not perfect and the boy still misbehaves now and then. He is doing better in school, i.e., closer to school's and parents' expectations in terms of grades. The parents still sometimes think that this misbehavior is a symptom of some problem or another, but nonetheless, for over six months they have not felt the need for additional therapy.

Pretending that the ~~problem~~ is solved, that there has been a miracle, allows the boy to save face: Pretending is only makebelieve. That is, he can change without having to admit that his parents had been right about there having been a ~~problem~~. He can change without changing because he is only pretending. When the therapist, parents, peers, and school personnel respond in a favorable manner, then he can forget to pretend.

The young man pretended the ~~problem~~ was solved in order

to confuse and trick his parents who thought he had a problem even though he did not think he had one. In this case, his goal was to get his parents off his back, and the way he did that was first to pretend to have a problem so that he could then act as if it was solved. That is, the parents saw their son as having a problem. The son did not see that problem, but he felt that his parents were needlessly on his back. He solved the problem of getting his parents off his back, which accidentally solved the parents' problem.

CASE EXAMPLE SIX: ONLY AN EXPERIMENT

[Unit 51] Therapist[6]: . . . you wake up in the morning and it dawns on you that there's been a miracle; the process is over. How would you know that?

[52] Client: It would be similar to the onset. It's not like a switch, it's in stages.

[53] T: I was thinking about when the stages are all done.

[54] C: I mean, it might be over the period of a week that I realize it's all over instead of one particular point in time.

[55] T: In the course of that week, what will be the signs?

[56] C: I would be able to laugh a lot easier.

[57] T: OK.

[58] C: . . . would be rid of anxieties I'm facing right now . . . at that point, I'll be externalizing my feelings towards my job . . . and I guess the big thing will be when I made up my mind: Do I want to stay or not? Either way, there will have to be an answer to this whole thing, to be able to say with real positive feelings, that "Yes I want to stay, doing what I'm doing" or "No, I'm not going to stay and I'm going to start looking for something else."

[59] T: OK.

[60] C: I'll have reached the point where I'm starting to

---

[6]Steve de Shazer

run toward something rather than away from something.

[61] T: Right ... anything else? (*pause*) How would your wife know?

[62] C: (*long pause*) She'd know when I go back to, you know, when I said I'll laugh more easily, having a better time and not being as serious. Kind of taking things with a grain of salt more than I did. That might be one of the ways.

[63] T: OK. What else?

[64] C: She'd love it if I stopped snoring — but I don't think that has anything to do with it — is snoring stress related?

[65] T: I don't know. I hope not. What else will she notice?

[66] C: At the same time I'm appearing to be happier and being able to enjoy myself, she'd see my regaining my ability to make decisions and to say "Yes" or "No" to things, to say "I'm going to do this" or "I'm going to do that" instead of "I'm really not sure. ..."

The client did not know whether he was depressed, was suffering through a mid-life crisis, was just getting old, was unhappy with his job, or was "unconsciously unhappy" with his marriage. He hoped that it was not the marriage that was bugging him because he thought he loved his wife and she loved him. He said he felt a vague, unexplicit, unintelligible dissatisfaction or emptiness. The more he thought about it, the more confused he became about (a) what the problem might be, (b) what the cause might be, (c) the fact that it might be a combination of some of the possibilities, and (d) that it might be some totally different undiscovered problem.

A therapist could focus on the complaint and try to help the client construct one or more of the possibilities into a solvable problem. But developing a solution by focusing on the possibility of a miracle bypasses that and allows for the possibility of "solving more than one ~~problem~~, all at the same time." Or, to put it another way, "You never know what ~~problem~~ you are solving when you develop a solution." Regardless, the miracle question and the clients' response allow for disconnecting the solution process from the ~~problem/complaint~~ even when the complaint is unnamed, vague, and ephemeral. The distinction between ~~problem/complaint~~ and nonproblem/complaint can still be utilized to develop a solution-focused language game even when the ~~problem/complaint~~ is unknown. At times, the client's not knowing what the problem is can be used to help the client deconstruct the complaint.

> T: We're impressed with how well you are handling not knowing. To us, too, it is a puzzle. If it's any one of them, you're handling it quite well, but if it's any combination of them, you are doing far better than we would have expected.
>
> Now that we are beginning to know what you are running toward, we have an experiment that might help you sort things out.
>
> Each night, before you go to bed, we want you to toss a coin. The first and third times it comes up heads, we want you, throughout the whole next day, to pretend the miracle has happened, the whole process is over and you've made the decision to stay. The second and fourth times it comes up heads, we want you, the next day, to pretend the process is over and you've made the decision to not stay. When it comes up tails you don't have to pretend anything.
>
> Observe how you feel, what you do, what your wife notices – this coin-toss-pretending should be secret from her – see how she responds, etc.

experiment, a test or trial of something; specifically, **(a)** any action or process undertaken to discover something not yet known . . . **(b)** something tried to find out whether it will be effective. to try; also, to establish by trial.

Of course, the solution is not yet known and, although the client's description of the day after the miracle is not very concrete, it is quite specific in comparison to his descriptions earlier in the session. It is enough for him to begin to invent what the solution will look like without having to worry about what the ~~problem~~ might have been.

Wittgenstein talks about experiments for showing someone what a word or a concept means:

> What is fear? What does "being afraid," mean? If I wanted to define it at a single shewing [sic] — I should *play-act* fear. . . . Describing my state of mind (of fear, say) is something I do in a particular context. (Just as it takes a particular context to make a certain action into an experiment). (Wittgenstein, 1958, p. 188).

Clearly, if defining "fear" through showing can be done in an experiment, then play-acting that the problem has been solved, that the solution has been invented and the goal achieved within the context of client's everyday life, can sometimes be enough to show the client that the goal has been reached. More usually, it is enough for the client to *show* himself what the goal is, enough to define the goal in manageable, realistic, behavioral terms. Locating the experiment in the client's day-to-day context is crucial for showing him what the solution is going to look like, feel like, and be perceived like by others.

Thus, "pragmatics," the study of the relationship between words and other behaviors, is also "pragmatic" in that words can be used to lead to practical results, to more satisfactory or useful behaviors, thoughts, feelings, and perceptions (in the client's life outside of therapy) that the client can report in subsequent sessions. It is only through the practical results depicted by the client that the client and the therapist alike can know that therapy was useful to the client.

11

HOW CAN WE KNOW WHEN TO STOP MEETING LIKE THIS?
Case Example Seven

> *The object [of therapy] is to get the client out of therapy and actively and productively involved in living his or her life.*
>
> —*Dolan, 1985, p. 29*

The view of therapy as a set of language games, as a linguistic system focused on developing solutions, is related to, but distinct from, an orientation toward therapy developed by Anderson and Goolishian (1988). Rather than focusing on solutions or solution-determined systems, Anderson and Goolishian focus on "problem-determined systems" and thus develop a perspective that organizes itself around the idea that "the therapeutic system is a problem-organizing, problem-dis-solving system" (p. 372):

Therapy is a linguistic activity in which being in conversation about a problem is a process of developing new meanings and understandings. The goal of therapy is to participate in a conversation that continually loosens and opens up, rather than constricts and closes down. Through therapeutic conversation, fixed meanings and behaviors (the sense people make of things and their actions) are given room, broadened, shifted, and changed. *There is no other required outcome.* (Anderson & Goolishian, 1988, p. 381) [Emphasis added]

Anderson and Goolishian seem to be using a definition developed by Giacomo and Weissmark (1987):

> [There] are three ways of dealing with conflict, and these correspond to ways of dealing with problems in general: solution, resolution, and dissolution. . . . *To dissolve a problem, the conditions that generate the dichotomy are changed so that it disappears.* (p. 456) [Emphasis added]

But . . . what about what the client wants to get out of therapy? After all, what the client wants is what counts. Once the problem dis-solves, what takes its place?

As opposed to the "problem-organizing problem-dis-solving" approach, in the solution[1]-determined approach, ~~problem~~ is always already dis-solved by the depiction of exceptions, of some precursors of the goal, of the *possibility* of exceptions via depictions of imagined or hypothetical solutions. Problem dis-solving (i.e., ~~problem~~) is just the starting point[2].

> **solution,** 1: the act, method, or process of solving a problem. 2: an explanation, clarification, answer, etc.; as, the solution of a mystery.
> The *Thesaurus* lists: answer, explanation, interpretation, key, clue. *syn.* conclusion, culmination, denouement, outcome, resolution, result, answer, key.

In solution-focused therapy or solution-determined conversations, the client's goal achievement signals to client and therapist alike that a solution is developing or has developed. This

---

[1]Giacomo & Weissmark (1987) use a definition of "solution" that is far different from that used by solution-focused therapists. For us, "solution" is what begins to develop once the problem is dis-solved and what happens once the client's goal is met.

[2]Post-structural constructions are not necessarily organized and focused on solutions and are not necessarily termination determined activities. For instance, it is clear that Anderson and Goolishian (1990) continue the traditional therapeutic focus on problems, and Hoffman (1990), who labels her work as "postmodern," also continues to conceptualize her work traditionally, i.e., around complaints. However, in neither case is it clear what they and their clients do when they are doing therapy.

means the end of therapy. Therapists are hired by clients to do a job for them, even though

> it is the clients' responsibility to tell us [therapists] about the changes they wish to see occur, we [therapists] take a very active role to assure that the goals are attainable and, hopefully, concrete enough so that we will know when we get there. This goal-setting procedure is very definitely a cooperative negotiation process. Our [the therapists'] active role in this aspect of therapy maximizes the chances that client will accomplish the goals constructed. (O'Hanlon & Weiner-Davis, 1989, p. 101)

Simply, "the goal [in solution-focused brief therapy] is best thought of as some member of the class of ways that the therapist and client will know that the problem is solved rather than any particular member of that class" (de Shazer, 1988, p. 93).

The majority of a solution-determined therapeutic conversation is spent in language games focused on three interrelated activities:

1. Producing exceptions and/or prototypes (examples of the goal(s) in clients' lives that point to desired changes),
2. imagining and describing new lives for clients, and
3. "confirming" that change is occurring, that clients' new lives have indeed started.

~~PROBLEM, CAUSALITY~~

The concept "problem" always presupposes the concept of "solution." In fact, the concept of solution is a precondition essential for the development of a concept of problem. Otherwise, what is called a "problem" (i.e., a depiction of an undesirable state of affairs requiring the doing of something) would be simply a "fact," just a depiction of *the way things are.*

Since the beginning, in the therapeutic discourse, "problem" has always held a privileged, primary position. The structure and etiology of problems have been the traditional focus of therapeutic discourse from Freud to Selvini Palazzoli, in part, due to the dominance of structural ways of thinking and, in part, due to the tendency to see the kinds of problems that therapists deal with as analogous to the kinds of problems (diseases) dealt with in physical medicine. That is, if the problem is seen as a disease, it obviously has a cause.

And thus, the structualists focus on the so-called dysfunctions of the family system. When the methodological boundary is drawn around the family system and thus system is a substitute for psyche, then – in spite of the emphasis in systems theory on circular causality, equifinality, and multifinality – the result is linear causality, a mechanical model, i.e., a dysfunctional system leads to symptoms.

However, when the methodological boundary is drawn around the therapeutic system, and the concepts of equifinality and multifinality are brought into play and used as two of the descriptive tools, then it seems easier to reject the concept of causality outright than it is to describe how the therapist and the client mutually shape their joint endeavor.

This is not to say that in human affairs there are no such things as "causes." It only says that at least within the context of systems theory "specific causes" cannot be known and therefore the concept of ~~causality~~ might be set aside as having been found not very useful.

From the start, the concept of ~~causality~~ was necessarily distinguished from "noncausality" or causelessness.

> **causeless,** 1. having no apparent cause. 2. without adequate ground, reason, or motive.

This, of course, leaves us with doubt and uncertainty, a reality that needs to be constructed.

CONSTRUCTING SOLUTIONS

> There must not be anything hypothetical in our considerations. We must do away with all *explanation*, and description alone must take its place. . . . These are, of course, not empirical

problems; they are solved, rather, by looking into the workings of our language, and that in such a way as to make us recognize those workings: *in despite of* an urge to misunderstand them. The problems are solved, not by giving new information, but by arranging what we have always known. [It] is a battle against the bewitchment of our intelligence by means of language. (Wittgenstein, 1958, #109)

With the concepts of ~~causality~~ and ~~problem~~ held in abeyance and surrounded by doubt, solution-determined conversations help clients describe and orient their lives in new ways. Therapist and clients together enter into the language game of goal definition, thereby creating the social and interactional conditions for producing progressive narratives focused on change and goal achievement.

CASE EXAMPLE SEVEN: THE WRONG TASK

At the very beginning of the session, before the therapist had said anything, before, in fact, all three people were sitting:

[Unit 1] Mrs. Q: That experiment we were supposed to do? We never got an opportunity.

[2] Mr. Q: We were going to, but . . .

[3] Therapist[3]: (Interrupting) Well, let's start from . . . so, what's better?

Units 1 and 2 show the start of a problem-focused language game; unit 3 shows the therapist's first attempt to start a solution-focused language game, as he tries to elicit news of difference or change (Gingerich, de Shazer, & Weiner-Davis, 1988).

[4] Mr. Q: We haven't really had any problems. The average three spats a week . . . we cut 'em off though.

[5] Mrs. Q: Yeah, we do.

[6] T: How do you do that?

[3]Steve de Shazer

[7] Mr. Q: A few times, just by me walking away.

[8] Mrs. Q: Yeah.

[9] T: OK.

[10] Mrs. Q: I just let it go too.

[11] Mr. Q: Just let 'em go and they die.

[12] Mrs. Q: And later on, we start talking to each other again.

[13] T: That works better?

[14] Mr. Q: Yeah, it works better . . .

[15] Mrs. Q: . . . than standing there screaming at each other. We should be able to just talk to each other.

Simon et al. (1985) suggest

> that how family therapists deal with the various forms of resistance, whether by an individual or by the united efforts of an entire family, depends both on the circumstances involved and on the theory and techniques of the therapist. In general, family therapists try simultaneously to maintain control of the situation and be flexible in their intervention strategies, yet at the same time to "go along" with the family's resistance, in other words, to avoid at all costs an escalation of resistance that would result from "resisting the resistance." In this respect, Erickson hypnotherapy has been of central importance. (Simon et al., 1985, p. 298)

For example, Erickson was quite clear about his revolutionary view of resistance as responsiveness: "You suggest that they withhold [resist]—*and they do.* And you also suggest that they tell you—*and they do.* But they withhold [resist] and they tell you responsively. And as long as they are going to withhold, *you ought to encourage them to withhold* [resist]" (Erickson quoted in Haley, 1973, p. 97). And Erickson also says that

> any of the possibilities constitute responsive behavior. Thus a situation is created in which the subject can express his resistance in a constructive, cooperative fashion; manifestation of resistance by a subject is best utilized by developing a situation in which resistance serves a purpose. (Erickson in Haley, 1967b, p. 20)

The "inside" of the concept of resistance is defined as just about anything that gets in the way of initiating or completing therapy, but what is on the "outside" of the distinction? An antonym suggested by the thesaurus is "cooperation." Interestingly, "cooperation," this "outside" of the concept of resistance, was actually part of what was "inside" Erickson's concept of resistance. Once again we can see a concept deconstruct.

At BFTC

> we found that accepting nonperformance [of tasks] as a message about the clients' way of doing things (rather than as a sign of resistance) allowed us to develop a cooperating relationship with clients. (de Shazer, 1985, p. 21).

[16] T: You're doing it [talking to each other] sometimes now.

In units 3 through 16, therapist and clients are negotiating: Is this a complaint-focused language game with stability and digressive narratives or a solution-focused language game with the therapist eliciting and attempting to amplify all differences mentioned (units 4 through 16, particularly units 13, 14, 15); in other words, is it change talk or solution talk?

[17] Mrs. Q: Yeah, but it has to start with an argument. When we disagree, we should be able to just sit down and talk about it.

[18] T: What else is different, better from your point of view?

[19] Mrs. Q: Everything is just about the same. I don't think anything's really improved. I don't know if that's because we didn't do the experiment and that's why nothing's changed.

Units 17 and 19, which include a stability narrative, show a problem-focused language game for the last time in the session.

[20] T: You haven't had any big blowups . . . That's different.

At unit 20, the therapist again tries to elicit talk of change and difference and continues to amplify, to help the clients expand on the examples.

[21] Mrs. Q: It was only two weeks.
[22] T: Didn't you usually have at least one in a two-week period?
[23] Mrs. Q: We did have one small one that could have . . .
[24] Mr. Q: . . . progressed into a big one.
[25] T: But it didn't.
[26] Mrs. Q: We just let it go. I 'spose that was a triumph for us.
[27] T: Yeah. That sounds different. How did you do that?
[28] Mrs. Q: I just stopped.
[29] T: How did you get yourself to stop?
[30] Mrs. Q: I told myself to stop.
[31] T: And you listened to yourself.
[32] Mrs. Q: I guess I did.
[33] T: But, what about him? It takes two to fight.
[34] Mrs. Q: He walked away. When I shut up, then he walked away. I usually go on and on.
[35] T: OK. You shut up, he let you do that. He walked away, and you let him do that. And that's how you prevented what might have been a big blowup from becoming one. That sounds different to me. (*long pause*) If you were to do that with other things – would that be minimally sufficient? Not perfect, but OK?
[36] Mr. Q: Yeah, it would be.

It turns out that Mr. and Mrs. Q were actually talking about two separate and distinct episodes and in the course of the session they described three additional examples that followed a similar pattern.

During the previous session, Mr. and Mrs. Q had described various ways they would know the problem was solved, but these ways were not very well defined or specific, and thus as a group they were given the name "10." The therapist used a scale to simplify and to help define the goal:

[111] T: If "10" stands for the goal, any or all of what you've just been talking about, not perfection but just having things as good as you two can make them, and "0" stands for where things were when things were at the worst they were, where do you think your husband is today between "10" and "0"?

[112] Mrs. Q: "5."

[113] T: And where do you think she is today?

[114] Mr. Q: "5."

[116] T: Did you both guess right?

[117] Mr. and Mrs. Q: Yeah.

In the current session (the session described in this chapter), after more descriptions of the "shut up, walk away and talk later" pattern, which included a rather clear description of how they both prepared to talk when it came time to talk, and before the therapist consulted with the team:

[37] T: Where are you on that "goal scale" we talked about last time?

[38] Mrs. Q: "7."

[39] Mr. Q: "8."

Units 20 through 36 show a solution focus with a progressive narrative and this progressive narrative continues into the goal-focused language game, units 111 through 117 and 37 through 39.

Remember: These are clients who started off the session by reporting nonperformance of the homework task (which some therapists would have seen as resistance), reporting that "*everything is just about the same. I don't think anything's really improved. I don't know if that's because we didn't do the experiment and that's why nothing's changed.*" Subsequently they report having "improved," for him from "5" to "8" and for her from "5" to "7." And, they agreed that if there were to use the same approach in other disagreements, that approach would be *minimally sufficient.*

When implementing the concept of cooperation,

First we connect the present to the future (ignoring the past [except past successes]), then we compliment the clients on what they are already doing that is useful and/or good for them, and then – once they know we are on their side – we can make a suggestion for something new that they might do which is, or at least might be, good for them. (de Shazer, 1985, p. 15)

And thus we used the following intervention which, like all interventions, was designed to serve as a context marker, to distinguish between ~~problem/complaint~~ and solution.

[40] T: As we[4] thought about this, I'm actually – it turns out – glad to hear that you did not do the experiment. Because what you two actually did together actually worked far better. And, I'm not even sure that the experiment would have helped as much as what you guys did – so, just forget it: It was clearly the wrong thing to suggest.

   It seems to us that you two simply need to continue doing what you've done these past weeks. It seems to us that you've got a good model to follow: It's working for you. It's a good pattern to follow and we think that – as it continues to work – you'll develop a lot more confidence in it.

Unit 40 sums up the solution-focused language game as it has developed so far. Notice the team's acceptance of the fact that the clients did not do the previous homework assignment and how that is turned into part of the solution-focused language game. Not only in this particular case, but in all cases,

[4]Other members of the team were Larry Hopwood and Mark Taylor.

what the clients actually *did* to make things "better" is more important than task performance. The implicit message in any task is, of course: Do something to make things better.

* * *

Where you can't look for an answer, you can't ask either, and that means: Where there's no logical method for finding a solution, the question does not make sense either.

Only where there's a method of solution is there a problem (of course that doesn't mean "Only when the solution has been found is there a problem"). That is, where we can only expect the solution from some sort of revelation, there isn't even a problem. A revelation doesn't correspond to any question. (Wittgenstein, 1975a, #149)

Solution-determined therapy necessarily results in narratives that are designed to confirm whether or not satisfactory change has occurred and/or is occurring. Beginning with the second session and continuing until the final session, the primary conversation activity focuses around the question "What is better?" "Better" is, of course, a family resemblance type of concept, so that the best way to answer the question is by pointing to a series of examples, as the couple and the therapist did in this session. Progressive narratives are useful in constructing a solution; stability and/or digressive narratives are not useful, and therefore the therapist wants to open the interview by simply asking the client "What is better?" rather than "How did the homework go?" or some other specific question. In this way, the range of possible progressive narratives in response is expanded to include anything and everything the clients view as making their lives more satisfactory. Clear-cut criteria for both success and failure can be difficult to establish because neither success nor failure is an entity or specimen. Instead we point at a series of examples — as in this session — and/or develop somewhat arbitrary operational definitions (i.e., "10" on a goal scale).

Clients' descriptions of complaints, exceptions, and goals are distinct language games, products of the interaction between therapists and clients. As can be seen from this example, what the clients come to see as worth describing is influenced and shaped by the therapists' part in the dialogue. The therapist's focus on constructing a solution or on progressive narratives helps the clients reorient themselves toward seeing what they have already accomplished.

Goal achievement provides a major theme around which clients and therapists organize descriptions of change and solution. Once the clients are confident that the goal has been achieved and that the changes involved are likely to continue, then both therapists and clients can know that they can stop meeting.

12

AT WORK
Case Example Eight

Only where there's a method of solution is there a problem.

— Wittgenstein, 1975, #149

In the previous chapters, verbatim excerpts from various cases were used to illustrate the different aspects of the solution-focused therapeutic conversation as progressive narratives and solution determined language games. Each of these quotations was, unfortunately, cut off from the whole of the conversation. Thus you, as reader, could not get a sense of the development of the session's conversation from start to finish. Even though some sections had to be eliminated to protect the clients' confidentiality, it is hoped that the following verbatim transcript will provide you with some grasp of the flow of a session.

The framework developed in the previous chapters allows us to see any therapy session as a purposeful conversation, which – like any other conversation – is shaped by the interactions of the participants. Therapy sessions involve progressive, regressive, and/or stability narratives and various language games, regardless of the content. Once the conversation and the language games are seen as the system of concern to therapists (rather than the inferred or hypothetical systems frequently focused on by therapists), then any conversation can be viewed as following the rules of systems.

CASE EXAMPLE EIGHT: BUILDING HALOS OF THE RIGHT SIZE AND RIGHT COLOR

Session #1

After finding out the employment situations of Mr. and Mrs. W:

[8] Therapist[1]: What shall I call you?
[9] Ralph.
[10] Sandy.
[11] R: May I call you Steve?
[12] T: Right. What brings you two in today?
[13] S: We're having serious marital problems.
[14] T: Of what sort?
[15] R: We keep thinking of having a divorce. Ah. She runs away or I send her away and she goes where her folks are and, (*pause*)
[16] T: OK, but somehow you get back together again?
[17] R: Yeah. We love each other dearly, we say. Do you love me dearly? I love you dearly. (*She reaches for his hand.*)
[18] T: OK, so let's imagine—it's going to be difficult but—let's imagine that there's a miracle some night while you two are sleeping and the problem that brings you here is solved. OK? While you're sleeping, so you don't know it's happened. What, the next day, what would be happening? What will tell you that this problem is solved?

(*Long pause*)

Using the miracle question this early in the first session is an attempt to establish the solution-focused language game, with a progressive narrative, as the primary focus of the session.

---

[1]Steve de Shazer with Insoo Kim Berg, Larry Hopwood, Jane Kashnig, and Scott Miller behind the mirror.

[19] R: Her depression would be over. I'd stop hearing auditory hallucinations and we'd be having intercourse frequently and enjoying it.

[20] T: OK. How about you?

[21] S: He'd stop telling me what to do and he would talk to me more often. He'd pay attention to me.

[22] T: OK.

[23] S: (*Crying*) I'm sorry.

[24] T: That's OK. I expect you two to disagree with each other. That's normal. That's the way marriages are. It's how you handle disagreements that counts.

You say that her depression would be over. How would you know it was over? What would she be doing that will tell you "It's over"?

[25] R: She'd stop crying and she'd be happy.

[26] T: What would she do instead of cry?

[27] R: Redirect her life into things she wants to do.

[28] T: Like what, for instance?

[29] R: . . . Help me earn a living, throw money into the pot.

[30] T: OK. What else will be different that you'll notice?

[31] S: We'll have intercourse more often.

[32] R: Yeah.

[33] T: More often? How much would be more often?

[34] R: We've had it once this month and we've tried every trick in the book. We had intercourse three times last month. It's becoming less and less frequent. I seem to be interested in every woman except Sandy.

[35] T: So, more frequently would be more than three times a month you say?

[36] R: Yes.

From unit 18 through unit 36, a progressive narrative develops quickly, promoted by the early use of the miracle question. During this conversation, a measurable goal of their having intercourse more than three times a month has been established. Other potential ways to know the solution has been developed have been mentioned: (a) Her depression would be over, (b) he would stop hearing voices, (c) he would stop telling her what to do, (d) they would be talking more together, and (e) she would stop crying so much.

[37] S: (*Simultaneously*) Yes. He stays out late a lot at night and that's been a problem lately. Sometimes he has to unwind, so he's out after midnight, which I understand. I don't mind. But sometimes he stays out pretty late and then he sleeps in in the morning and so I'm already in bed when he comes home. So, it's hard to wake me up and have intercourse.

[38] T: So, you have a scheduling problem there. (*pause*)

[39] T: So, that would be different. What else will be different? When you're no longer depressed, what will you be doing?

[40] S: Umm. (*pause*) I'd be working, pursuing my career. It's been dragging out, me getting in applications, but I've been to three places, so I've started.

[41] T: When did you start?

[42] S: A couple of weeks ago.

[43] T: A couple of weeks. OK, you've got that started. Good. Good.

(*Pause*)

[44] T: You also said something about, something else.

[45] R: Voices.

[46] T: Voices.

Units 39 through 46 continue the progressive narrative. Not only has a measure of success been described, but she has already started to do something about finding a job and/or furthering her career.

[47] R: Auditory hallucinations and delusions of reference. I've had 'em for 20 years. The diagnosis —

[48] T: (*Interrupting*) Just a minute. Wait with that. Let me find out something else first. After this miracle, what will be different about that?

[49] R: They'd all be gone.

[50] T: They'll all be gone. When was the most recent time when they were gone?

[51] R: (*Long pause*) They're gone now.

[52] T: They're gone now. And how long have they been gone?

[53] R: (*Long pause*) I don't know.

[54] T: OK.

[55] R: I think I hear them when I'm bored.

[56] T: Sure. They've been gone for some time? Days? Months? Weeks? What?

(*Long pause*)

[57] S: Did you hear them last night when we went out to eat?

[58] R: Yes. Delusions of reference. I take medications for them the psychiatrist prescribed and that helps . . . but I . . .

[59] T: But they're gone right now?

[60] R: Yes.

[61] T: Since you got up this morning?

[62] R: Yes.

[63] T: How come they're gone like that sometimes? What's different when they're gone?

(*Long pause*)

[64] T: Well, think about that for a minute. Do you know when they're gone?

[65] S: No. He's not more talkative when they're gone. I thought that he would be, but that doesn't seem to be the case.

[66] T: Is he more physically active when they're gone?

[67] R: I'm able to think. I'm able to think. Otherwise, I have to keep a "to do list" and I have to tell myself "I hear my thoughts." I'm not able to read or retain.

(*Pause*)

[68] R: Is it really this simple?

[69] T: It might be.

[70] R: OK. Good. Good.

In unit 47, Ralph, who is familiar with talking in a certain way about his voices to therapists, begins a stability narrative.[2] But, unit 48 turns that around, and the progressive narrative continues to develop through unit 64, even though there are times (unit 58 for instance) when Ralph's usual way of talking about his voices slips back in.

In order for a solution to develop and to develop quickly, a solution-focused progressive narrative needs to be maintained with clients who are used to other approaches to therapy. It is all too easy to join in the exploration of history and causal hypothesis-building.

[88] T: When was the most recent time you weren't feeling depressed or were not aware of feeling depressed?

[89] S: It's been a long time.

[90] T: About when? When was the most recent day when you were less depressed than today?

[91] S: Hmmm. (*Long pause*) A couple of years ago.

[92] T: Is that right? What do you think? When was the most recent day you thought she was less depressed?

[93] R: It was in the last two months. You had a happy day: You were shopping and looking for a job. You had just returned and you were elated. I was working: You got rid of me!

(*Both laugh*)

[94] T: Maybe. Is that right? Had you forgotten that day? Or is it just his perception?

[95] S: I don't know.

[96] T: It could be either?

[97] S: Yeah.

[98] T: But he thinks so.

[99] R: She seemed to be happy, she was smiling.

Units 88 through 99 perhaps point to an exception and at least start to build some doubt about Sandy's perception that she has been uniformly depressed for years.

---

[2]Later in the session, we learn more about Ralph's experience, which includes the fact that for "14 years I've been in therapy for my voices" and Sandy was in therapy for nine years about her "obsessive-compulsive illness."

[100] T: Does that have any effect on the voices?
(*Long pause*)
[101] R: I think I take advantage of her happiness.
[102] T: What do you mean?
[103] R: I kind of abuse her when she's happy.
[104] T: In what sense?
[105] R: In order to gain control.
[106] T: I'm not understanding, what do you mean? (*Long pause*) How do you go about that?
[107] R: I get angry with her when she's happy, 'cause I'm not happy and I'm spent. I guess when she's happy it doesn't help my voices.
[108] T: OK, or increase 'em either?
[109] R: No, no.

Units 100 through 109 suggest the need for more specific, behavioral questions when talking with Ralph.

[110] T: When was the most recent time the two of you had a good day at the same time?
(*Long pause*)
[111] R: It hasn't been all that bad, has it?
(*Sandy is crying.*)
[112] T: She thinks so.
(*Long pause*)
[113] S: We sat down and talked with his mother the other day and Ralph has improved his behavior toward me. He hasn't ordered me around as much. And, yeah. He's been more considerate.

Units 110 and into the start of 113 looks like it is going to be another regressive or stability narrative, but Sandy's switch in 113 points to an exception. Here is another example of a client's depiction of change.

[114] T: Since, when did this start?
[115] S: Two days ago.
[116] T: Two days ago.

[117] S: We had a conversation with his mother. We sat down and talked.

[118] T: Are you aware that you've been changing your behavior over the past couple of days?

[119] R: It's a conscious effort.

[120] T: Good. Good. (*Shakes Ralph's hand. Both Sandy and Ralph smile.*) And it's been a successful effort.

[121] R: Yes, yes.

[122] T: And that makes life easier for you, and you.

[123] R: For her.

[124] T: What about for you? As a result of your conscious and deliberate efforts, it makes it better for her. Will it make it better for you then?

[125] R: It should.

[126] T: Has it yet?

[127] R: No, not yet.

[128] T: Not yet.

[129] R: She's a little happier though. (*Sandy nods.*)

[130] T: OK. It might start to pay off pretty soon.

[131] R: Yes.

[132] T: Has it been a lot of work or just some?

[133] R: No, just a little.

Units 113 through 133 return to the progressive narrative and allow Ralph and the therapist to begin to construct a perception of a useful relationship between Ralph's behavior and Sandy's.

[133, continued] I'd been ordering her around a lot and I should be a gentleman. She's a lady and I should be a gentleman.

[134] T: Your legs aren't broken, so you can get up and do it yourself?

[135] R: Yes.

[136] T: And so you turned over a new leaf a couple of days ago and so—what has he done that you have appreciated most in the last couple of days?

[137] S: He hasn't ordered me around as much.

[138] T: What's he do instead?
[139] S: He's been asking me, "How was your day?"
[140] T: And what else?
[141] S: "What did you do at work?"

The progressive narrative continues through 141 and the interaction between Sandy's behavior and Ralph's new behavior becomes clearer. A subplot or even a whole language game about the "ease" of change has begun to develop. Ralph's new behaviors over the previous two days can be seen as exceptions that are clearly related to Sandy's goals. This may be one of the threads that can be used to unravel the whole complaint or a loose stone that can be used to deconstruct the the ~~problem~~ and thus to promote the construction of a solution.

[141, continued] We're still having trouble with long silences. But I don't know if Ralph was ever real talkative.
[142] T: How long have you two been together?
[143] S: Seven years.
[144] R: Married seven, known each other nine.
[145] T: So, how long is a long silence?
[146] R: We're quiet at the dinner table when we're by ourselves. When we're with mom, I talk to mom, mom talks to Sandy, Sandy talks to mom, mom talks to me. When we are by ourselves, we're very quiet. I don't know what to say.
[147] T: OK. I guess I'm wondering, these silences. Are you thinking that there's something that should be said during that silence and you're holding it back or is it that there's nothing to be said right then?
[148] S: I don't know. Maybe there's nothing to be said.
[149] T: Maybe. Are you conscious of holding something back? Are you conscious of his holding something back?
[150] S: I'll say something to him sometimes and he won't respond. He's lost in his thoughts. I don't know if he's hearing voices at that time or not.

In units 141 through 150 the therapist attempts to induce some doubt about the "problematic" label attached to the silences.

[151] T: Right. (*pause*) That's interesting, the past couple of days, because of his doing some things differently, have you caught yourself doing things differently?

[152] S: No, I haven't, have I?

[153] T: You aren't aware of it at least.

[154] R: I just needed to change things. I don't want to order my wife around. That's rude. That's coarse. That's crude. It's a rut we were in and I'm thankful to be out of it.

[155] T: Is she responding with some different behavior also?

[156] R: She's much happier.

[157] T: OK.

Units 151 through 157 continue the development of a perception of a relationship between Ralph's new behavior and Sandy's responsive behavior.

* * *

[168] T: So, how do you think we can be of help to you? What are you looking for?

[169] R: I'd like to see, I'd like some help: I've never been able to give my wife an orgasm when we have intercourse and we'd like to increase the frequency of our intercourse.

[170] T: OK. That's the main thing you were thinking of, looking for getting here.

[171] R: And also, I'd like—we love each other, we care about each other.

[172] T: I can see that.

[173] R: Occasionally we talk divorce, occasionally we separate—but we are not prospering. That's the main

thing. That's the main beef my mom has with me, it's the main beef I have with me and with Sandy. We're not prospering. We're doing something wrong.

[174] T: Prospering would look like what?

[175] R: Being able to make ends meet.

[176] T: Economically.

[177] R: Yes.

[178] T: And what about you, what are you looking for?

[179] S: Trying to make up my mind about whether I should leave Ralph or not.

[180] T: And where are you on that today?

[181] S: I've been thinking about it again today. I'm sorry Ralph.

[182] R: I think of it too.

[183] T: So you are riding the fence.

[184] S: Yeah.

[185] T: And you're leaning which way?

[186] S: I don't know.

[187] T: And which way do you really want to lean?

[188] S: I don't know.

[189] T: How will you know? What will tell you, for instance, you want to stay?

[190] S: I'm not sure.

[191] T: Guess? It's a tough question.

[192] S: Ralph would be more successful in his work and in his personality.

[193] R: I really have been hard on her through the years. Not physically, emotionally. It's been tough for both of us.

[194] T: If these changes that he's making continue on, let's say six weeks from now, would that indicate something about which way to lean?

[195] S: It might.

Units 168 through 195 confirm the goals already described in response to the miracle question.

* * *

[203] T: What else do you think might help her make the decision to stay?

[204] R: If I could get my career moving again.

* * *

[260] T: Is there anything else I need to know at this point before I take some time to think about what you've been saying and talk with my team about what you've been saying that's useful? And then I'll come back and let you know what our thinking is. We've just scratched the surface so far.

At this point, both Sandy and Ralph sketch their "psychiatric" history. He had been given the diagnosis "paranoid schizophrenia," whereas she had been labeled as "obsessive-compulsive."

[270] R: I just want to be happily married.

[271] T: OK, I'll be back.

Intervention Message

[272] R: That didn't take so long.

[273] T: No. That's because you two were quite clear. It's clear to us that you've been through a lot, both individually and together. And, given what you've been through, we would have expected things to be much worse—which means to us that you two are doing some things quite right.

It's clear that, both individually and together, you want to make things better. As we were talking about this, we were really impressed with how much you care for each other and you both want to do what's good for each other. And that's not always clear with a lot of couples, but it's clear to us.

[274] R: Hear that!

[275] T: You know what to do and how to do it.

[276] R: We're doing something right.

(*They are smiling, looking at each other.*)

[277] T: Absolutely. And, the other thing that became very clear was that you've started to build a new life together.

We have some ideas, an experiment we'd like you two to do between now and next time we meet.

Each of you pick two days over the next week, secretly, and on those days, we want you to pretend that that miracle we talked about has already happened. OK?

And observe how the other person reacts to what you do. Then, see if you can figure out which two days she picks, you see if you can figure out which two days he picks. Don't say anything about it. Do it secretly, just observe. Observe how he reacts, observe how she reacts. You might even pick the same day by accident; that's OK. You might learn something extra that way. But it has to be by accident. It's got to be a secret; don't discuss it.

The team decided to use a "pretend the miracle has already happened" frame in an attempt to cover all the bases: (a) the end of Sandy's "depression," (b) the silence of Ralph's "voices," (c) an increase in the frequency of their sex life, (d) a continuation of the behavioral changes they had begun two days before the session, and, of course, (e) the start of anything else that might be part of a new life, anything else they say that makes things better for them.

Session #2

[1] T: So, what's better?

[2] S: Well, it was difficult for me to carry out the experiment because it was hard for me to stay high, to imagine that the miracle was happening for both him and me.

[3] T: Sure.

[4] S: You know what I mean? It was hard for me not to cry, not to be sad.

[5] T: Right, but during the times you were successful, how did it go?

Even a limited success with pretending might have made things better.

[6] S: I think that Ralph was more settled, he was less angry at me.

[7] T: OK, before I get to Ralph, just looking at the week as a whole, what was better?

[8] S: He told me what to do less often.

[9] T: That's continued. What else?

[10] S: And, ah, he was angry with me less.

[11] T: OK, what's he do when he's angry less? And he's ordering you around less? What does he do instead?

[12] S: Well, he's in his own world a lot of the time. (*pause*) I'm not sure what he does.

[13] T: Which two days do you think he picked to pretend?

[14] S: Thursday and Friday.

[15] T: All right. Which two days do you think she picked?

[16] R: Wednesday and Sunday.

[17] T: OK. Does that seem right?

(*Both laugh.*)

[18] R: This is fun.

[19] S: Which did he say?

[20] T: Wednesday and Sunday.

[21] R: Those were the days we had intercourse.

[22] T: Wonderful.

(*Both are smiling, laughing, and holding hands.*)

[23] T: Maybe she wasn't pretending those days.

[24] S: My days were Sunday and Monday.

[25] T: So, he was right about Sunday anyway. Ralph, she thought it was Thursday and Friday.

[26] R: It was Wednesday and Friday.

[27] T: Wednesday and Friday. Both of you were half right. Isn't that interesting?

Units 13 through 27, with six days involving either pretending or perceiving that a miracle had happened, give the clients and the therapist more material to use in building a solution.

> [28] R: I had no voices when I left your office. No auditory hallucinations. That lasted until lunch, when I got there . . .
>
> [29] T: They picked up again.
>
> [30] R: They picked up again.
>
> [31] T: What do you say, Ralph, about the week as a whole?
>
> [32] R: I talked with her a lot more often and I deliberately tried not to order her around more often. I think I only asked her to do maybe five things and, when I did, I was very careful to say "please" and "thank you," and the rest of the things I did myself. And that was easy to do.
>
> [33] T: It was easy?
>
> [34] R: It was easy.
>
> [35] T: How come it was easy? It's been a long habit of yours.
>
> [36] R: I've been wanting to change that for a long time.
>
> [37] T: Yeah, that would seem to me to make it even more difficult rather than easy. How come it was easy? Oh, well, that's just my puzzle.

Units 32 through 37, involving the ease of changing a long-term habit or pattern, continue the "easy change language game" which might help the therapist and the clients construct other "easy" changes.

> [38] R: We had intercourse twice. We only had it once last month.
>
> [39] T: So, already . . .
>
> [40] R: We're up two already.
>
> [41] T: My god, maybe there really was a miracle! (*All three are laughing.*) What else was better?

[42] S: I think he was angry less.

[43] T: That seems to fit.

[44] R: I was having more conversation with her. It was easier to talk to her.

Unit 44 points to another easy change. Later in the session it developed that their having had intercourse twice was also easy since they simply made a point of going to bed at the same (early) time.

Clearly, both Sandy and Ralph are depicting changes and thus the start of a new life.

[45] T: Good.

[46] R: And when I'm talking with her, I'm not hallucinating.

[47] T: Is that right?

[48] R: Yes.

[49] T: So, when you talk to her, there's no voices?

[50] R: Correct.

[51] T: Is it that, there's no voices and then you talk to her or you talk to her and there's no voices.

[52] R: Sometimes I talk with her and I get interrupted by the voices.

[53] T: Right.

[54] R: Or delusions of reference. I think people are talking to me or about me.

[55] T: Right, so there's a tendency that when you talk to her more, the voices are there less?

[56] R: Yeah. It's hard to make small talk and not talk about personal problems when in public.

[57] T: But you were doing that this week?

[58] R: Yeah, we were making small talk and having a good time with it.

[59] S: We were talking more.

Later in the session it becomes clear that this is the first time that Ralph sees a connection between talking with Sandy more and having less trouble with the voices.

[59, continued] It's very important, see, I don't get angry.

[60] T: You don't get angry or you don't show that you're angry.

[61] S: I don't get angry.

[62] T: You don't get angry, period?

[63] S: No, I just get frustrated.

[64] T: Oh.

[65] S: And, um, it hurts me very much when he gets angry at me.

[66] T: Right.

[67] S: I'm just throwing this out. It has nothing to do with what we were saying before.

[68] T: I was trying to figure that out.

[69] S: I'm just throwing this in, about our relationship. When Ralph gets terse, it hurts.

[70] T: So, you've been less frustrated this week.

[71] S: Yeah.

* * *

[200] T: Last time you were talking about having been depressed for a long time. Let's suppose that 10 stands for "back to normal" and "not depressed any more" and 0 is as bad, as depressed as you ever felt, where would you put yourself today?

[201] S: 4.

[202] T: 4, and last time you were here, where would you have put yourself?

[203] S: 0.

[204] T: 0! Somehow you've gotten from 0 to 4! How did you do that?

[205] S: I was at 0 for a few days, but Ralph wasn't angry at me, and that helped.

[206] T: Good. You worked together as a team.

[207] S: He helped me out.

[208] T: Did you know that she'd gone from 0 to 4?

[209] R: No.

[210] T: What would you have said if I'd have asked you first?

[211] R: About the same.

[212] T: Last week, he thought you were feeling better than you thought. Isn't that interesting? I don't know what to make of it.

[213] R: Let me know when you're happy.

[214] T: On the same kind of scale, with 10 standing for things being as well between the two of you as you can reasonably expect them to be, OK? And 0 is the pits, where would you put it today?

[215] R: 4.

[216] T: And you?

[217] S: 4.

[218] T: And how does that compare with last week?

[219] R: 0.

[220] S: 0, I would say too.

[221] T: The things you've been doing this past week have moved things from 0 to 4.

[222] R: I really believe this miracle can happen.

On Sandy's "depression scale" there had been a 4-point improvement and later in the interview we learn that on Ralph's "voice frequency scale" there had been a 1-point (10 to 9) improvement.

Intervention Message

[223] S: Before you say anything, I was just saying that I expect him to be a saint to me. I want him to be a saint, I want him to be kind to me all the time.

[224] T: Wouldn't that be nice?

[225] S: And it's hard for me.

[226] T: It's hard for him too.

[227] R: Trying for sainthood.

(*All laugh.*)

[228] R: But it's the wrong color halo (*pointing to the space above his head*).

[229] T: If you get a halo, that means she'll have one too.

[230] S: I'll have one too.

[231] T: As we see it, this week has been a new beginning

for both of you, building halos. Together, you've moved from 0 to 4. That's pretty significant, a 40% improvement.

[232] R: You come highly recommended.

[233] T: Yeah, but I didn't do anything. I just sit here and listen and talk sometimes, but you two are out there doing it—that's why the halos are starting to form.

Basically, you two need to continue doing the kinds of things you've been doing these past 10 days to make things better, even including pretending.

And, I think that I want to point out something the team told me about: When they see you two smiling, they see how you two really belong to each other.

[234] R: That's very kind of them. I've wondered if we should be married or not, and that helps me.

[235] T: I have an additional little task for you, a special kind of pretending: We'd like you to do an experiment and that is, if you're angry, we'd like you to pretend not to be.

[236] R: OK.

[237] T: And see what happens.

[238] R: OK.

*   *   *

By session five (eight weeks after session one),[3] after a period of rocky stability (ratings shifting between 3, 4, and 5), they reported that, not only had the frequency of sex increased, but their enjoyment of it had also increased. She was smiling more and feeling happier. Following a suggestion from session four, they found it rewarding for Ralph to hug Sandy when she was doing OK rather than comforting her when she was crying.

The frequency of Ralph's voices had declined from the peak at 10 to 4, with 0 (the goal) standing for silence. Ralph continued to find himself angry less often and he found that pretending not to be angry was effective "at

[3]The therapist in sessions 2 and 3 was Insoo Kim Berg.

least 95% of the time." As a couple, they rated the week before the fifth session as between 6 and 7 (with 10 as the goal) and she rated herself as at 7 (with 10 as the goal) on the "depression scale."

* * *

Although there has not been enough time to do a follow-up on this case, nonetheless, it is apparent that these conversations are following the patterns seen in a typical sequence of solution-focused therapy sessions. When therapist and clients focus the conversation on a solution-developing language game during the sessions, then the clients will frequently report on the construction and development of satisfactory solutions.

13

DIFFERENCE[1]

The elementary unit of information — is a difference which makes
a difference.

—Bateson, 1972, p. 453

What is this difference that I have attempted to put to work
throughout this book?

In the hard sciences, effects are, in general, caused by rather
concrete conditions or events — impacts, forces, and so forth.
But when you enter the world of communication, organization,
etc., you leave behind that whole world in which effects are
brought about by forces and impacts and energy exchange. You
enter a world in which "effects" — and I am not sure one should
still use the same word — are brought about by *differences*. That
is, they are brought about by the sort of "thing" that gets onto
the map from the territory. This is difference. (Bateson, 1972,
p. 452)

I have pointed to the obvious difference between one sign
and another, one concept and another, one word and another; to
the difference between the author's (intended) meanings and

---

[1] It must be remembered that I am not a philosopher by training and, therefore,
I want to apologize to any philosophers who might read this book and particularly this chapter for my simple-mindedness. I have taken from the philosophical discourse what I thought would be useful for this discourse, well aware that
I might have missed the philosophers' whole point. In particular, I want to
apologize to Ludwig Wittgenstein and Jacques Derrida for whatever abuse
they suffer at my hand.

the reader's meanings; and to the difference that is brought about by the moratorium on meaning (Derrida, 1978) brought about by, or even inherent in, these differences.[2] I hope that I have drawn a clear analogy between the situation of the author vis-à-vis the reader and the situation of the client and the therapist.

Bateson (1972) asks:

> But what is a difference? A difference is a very peculiar and obscure concept. It is certainly not a thing or an event. This piece of paper is different from the wood of this lectern. There are many differences between them — of color, texture, shape, etc. But if we start to ask about the localization of those differences, we get into trouble. Obviously the difference between paper and the wood is not in the paper; it is obviously not in the wood; it is obviously not in the space between them, and it is obviously not in the time between them. (Difference which occurs across time is what is call"change.")
>
> A difference, then, is an abstract matter. (p. 452)

Take, for instance, a short chain (sketched rather than fully drawn) developed from "difference": (see Figure 1). The chain of meanings attached to "difference" (developed from the dictionary and thesaurus), once situated in the brief therapy and family therapy discourses, could expand almost limitlessly once we take into account all the writings of Bateson, Weakland, Haley, etc. But all of the meanings attached to "difference" by author and reader are part of the meaning of "difference" brought into this specific context by both author and reader.

Rather than either indulging in free association or making a futile attempt to escape the entanglements of signs (as, for instance, the attempts of Austin (1976) and Searle (1970) to

---

[2]Derrida uses the word "differ*a*nce," including the silent writing of its *a* (a neologism of his own invention), to refer to difference (French *differer*) plus deference (Latin *differre*). Here he is pointing to the postponement, deferment, or delay of meaning and understanding in reading (or better, misreading, given the slipping and sliding), which is another kind of difference.

Figure 1. DIFFERENCE CHAIN

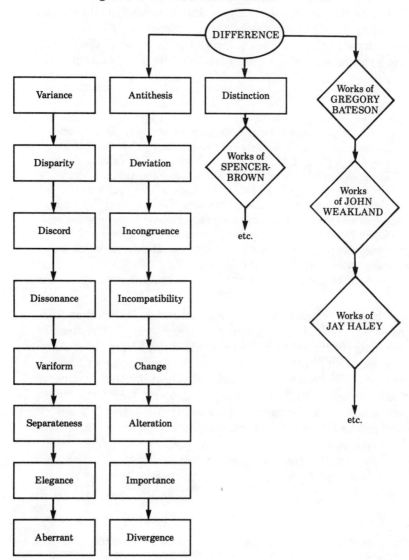

escape via "legislation"),[3] I have tried to point to the flexibility and creativity this difference provides for both therapist and client in the therapeutic situation. That is, if meaning is not seen as inherent or as locked into a word/concept, then Wittgenstein's idea that meaning can be determined by how the participants in a specific conversation in a certain context actually use the word/concept takes on a pragmatic and therapeutic usefulness. Since there is no certainty about word/concepts and meaning, cooperation – not competition – is the sine qua non of interactional constructivism. A language game is necessary to put constraints upon this infinite chain.

Locatability is, as Bateson says, problematic because difference is always difference *between*. In interactional constructivism, it is always a matter first of drawing a distinction (Spencer-Brown, 1973, p. 3): There is a difference between inside and outside. It is clear that difference has something to do with concepts having both an inside and an outside; it involves the distinction between map and territory and between "class" and "member." Difference has to do with the difference between concept and definitional criteria. But these boundaries are not barriers, they cannot be depended upon to keep inside and outside separate from each other. It is not simply that the difference between the inside and the outside of concepts and the permeability of boundaries can be used to develop a method of solution-focused brief therapy: It can be and has been done (de Shazer, 1988). It is equally clear that the difference between the inside and the outside of concepts, between various pairs of concepts, and between map and territory is not resolvable with some unifying third term; this difference is not a Hegelian contradiction. This difference is not simple, it is not a "something"; rather, it is a name for a relationship.

Perhaps a verb such as differentiating would have been more appropriate, but the phrase "putting differentiating to work" is, at best clumsy and awkward in English and might lead away

---

[3]This move is similar to that developed by Whitehead and Russell's theory of logical types (1910) where they tried to legislate against paradox.

from the chain of signs associated with "difference" that I wanted to invoke.

Instead, it is difference itself that is an important tool for therapists and clients. It is not simply that there are "differences which make a difference." In and of themselves, differences are just differences. Most frequently, differences do not work spontaneously. If they are not recognized, they make no difference, but once recognized, they can then be put to work to make a difference. Differences that count, differences that are significant to the client, are the effects or signatures of a difference put to work.

In the language game of therapy, the client's story makes the therapist see things one way; the therapist's revision (a difference) makes the client see things another way. If therapist and client cannot work it out, if they cannot put the difference to work, they are not negotiating; they are simply reacting to each other rather than replying. This brings us back to the pragmatics of doing therapy. The therapist needs to find a point, some element of the client's story that allows for difference being put to work. In any particular conversation that therapists and clients have, there are many possible points where a distinction can be marked, places where a difference can be pointed to. Any of these differences might be put to work toward making a difference so that the client can say that his or her life is more satisfactory.

14

EPILOGUE

The only ultimate truth is, "It all depends."

— Cyril Stanley Smith, 1978, p. 38

Every story, every book – whether murder mystery, philosophy, or technical manual – has to have an ending, or at least a strong sense of ending, a place where the author can say "I've done the best I can to say what I wanted to say, to say what I meant, and to mean what I said," and the reader can say "I got the whole story, I got the point of it all." At times, this ending can be ambiguous, like the ending of *Finnigan's Wake*, or artificial and contrived.

But, of course, the author reading his work misreads what he said: On one hand, the author always said more than he thought he said. On the other hand, the author's reading always reveals that he said less than he thought he said; and, of course, the book always turns out different from what the author wrote. Since the boundary is drawn around author-book-reader, each reading produces a new book; each rereading leads to new meanings, to another new book. And, therefore, the book is never finished, there is no end, just a sense of ending. (We know that when Sherlock Holmes retired from his detective work, he raised and studied bees. Ever wonder what Doctor Watson did when he retired?)

While I wonder what book you, the reader, have constructed with me, I can only know that I am satisfied with my part in it. Each author writes for a purpose (although it may seem to be a compulsion). The purpose of this book is to point to some ideas, some ways of thinking about doing therapy that to some readers may have at first appeared too radical or perhaps nonsensical. I hope the plot, although intricate, held the subplots together well enough so that you, as reader, were able to make some sense of things.

Of course you do not have to agree with what I said. That goes without saying (or it should go without saying, but it does not). I just hope that you and I were able to evolve enough cooperation, to take each other seriously, so that we were able to think about things together.

At the beginning, how could I expect you to take me seriously when I suggested that "nymphomania" is a word, just like any other word and that you, as reader, as well as I, as author, each have different meanings for that word and that whatever it is going to come to mean for us depends on some sort of negotiation? Constructivism (the idea that reality is invented rather than discovered) is bad enough, you might say, but interactional constructivism (the idea that reality is socially or interactionally invented) is even worse.

At least with (simple) radical constructivism, we can retain the spirit of the subject-object split and attribute clients' problems to their own constructive efforts, attributing any therapeutic failures to the problematic edifice they brought with them into therapy. However, with interactional constructivism it is not so easy. Therapeutic failures mean that both therapist and client have failed to construct a solution. The fault is on neither side while simultaneously it is on both sides. It takes at least two to fail at negotiation.

In the focused solution development model of brief therapy, failures seem most often to involve a breakdown of negotiation involving an answer to the question: How will we know when we can stop meeting like this? Too often the client is willing to accept the absence of the complaint as "goal enough," but the absence can never be proved and, therefore, success or failure cannot be known by either therapist or client. Unless clearly established through negotiations beforehand, even the presence of significant changes is not enough to prove the absence of the complaint.

Some failures can be seen as related to a difficulty in shifting from a "problem/complaint-focused language game" into a "solution-focused language game." This is, of course, another point at which the conversations between therapist-client can break down, when a digressive or stability narrative develops rather than a progressive narrative. The fault here is situated neither on the therapist's side nor on the client's side; both are in it together. Most frequently, failures that develop in this way mean that the therapist has been unable to help the client see exceptions as differerences that can be made to make a difference and thus as precursors of the goal, and/or the reversal of some hierarchical construction of meaning fell flat on its face because the reversal failed to make the meaning of the situation undecidable, and thus, the apparent difference did not make a difference to the client. In these situations, any intervention and any task based on the reversal will make no sense to the client, and the therapist (and therapy) will be dismissed as ineffective and perhaps irrelevant.

In some senses, the writing-reading of this book can fail in much the same way. Our negotiations about whether or not the differences I have put to work make any difference to you as reader may fail and the book may be dismissed as irrelevant to the purpose you had in reading it. That is, your goal for reading the book and my goal for writing it may have been too different and thus we failed to develop a joint work project.

This does not mean that you and I have to agree about things from one end of the book to the other! It only means that as author and reader we both have to reach our goals even though we have agreed to disagree. From my point of view, we can both reach our goals and continue to disagree about damn near everything as long as you came along for the journey, thinking about things in a different way, allowing yourself to let your mind wander around and to play with the differences put into play during this project.

APPENDIX I
Outcome Studies in Brief Therapy

As a non-normative therapy, brief therapists have always asked the client about success. After all, clients come to therapy to solve a problem and it is only they who can judge therapy's success. While this may not satisfy the utmost rigorous standards of pure (positivistic) research, it is certainly better than asking the therapist.

In a follow-up study at MRI, Weakland et al. (1974) reported a 72% success rate (40% complete relief of the presenting complaint and 32% clear and considerable improvement) within an average of seven sessions per case.

Giving lie to the old idea that brief therapy is just a band-aid or palliative approach, Fisher (1980) reported that six sessions were no more effective than 12 sessions and that there was a tendency for things to get better rather than worse subsequent to brief therapy (Fisher, 1984).

In our most recent follow-up at BFTC (Kiser, 1988; Kiser & Nunnally, 1990), using the same questions as those used by MRI to give us a standard and some addition questions, we found an 80.4% success rate (65.6% of the clients met their goal while 14.7% made significant improvement) within an average of 4.6 sessions. When recontacted at 18 months, the success rate had increased to 86%.

In addition, 77% reported no new problems had developed

and, in fact, 67% reported improvements in other areas since the end of therapy. Interestingly, 51.8% were seen for three sessions or less and they reported a 69.41% success rate while the 48.2% seen for four sessions or more reported a 91.14% success rate. Furthermore, when seen for three sessions or less 44.26% met a secondary goal while those seen for four sessions or more 61.29% met a secondary goal, a rather dramatic increase.

APPENDIX II

The most radical approach to time limits has been developed within a self-contained Health Maintenance Organization (Kaiser-Permanente) by Moshe Talmon (1990) who has developed a single session approach called Ultra-Brief Therapy.

In a totally different tradition, the usefulness of a single session in the treatment of alcohol abuse was shown (Edwards, Orford, Egert, Guthrie, Hawker, Hensman, Mitcheson, Oppenheimer, & Taylor, 1977; Orford, Oppenheimer, & Edwards, 1976; Zweben, Pearlman & Li, 1988). For instance, one hour of "brief advice giving" was compared with the state-of-the-art treatment including, both inpatient and outpatient with medication and AA. At follow-up after 12 and 24 months, both groups showed equal and significant improvement in alcohol consumption and symptom severity as well as in social adjustment (Orford et al., 1976).

REFERENCES

Ackerman, N. (1966). Family psychotherapy – Theory and practice. *American Journal of Psychotherapy, 20*: 405–414.

Anderson, H., & Goolishian, H. A. (1988). Human systems as linguistic systems: Preliminary and evolving ideas about the implications of clinical theory. *Family Process, 27(4)*: 371–393.

Anderson, H., & Goolishian, H. A. (1989). Dialogic rather than interventionist: An interview by L. Winderman, *Family Therapy News*, November/December.

Anderson, H., & Goolishian, H. (1990). Beyond cybernetics: Comments on Atkinson and Heath's "Further thoughts on second-order family therapy." *Family Process, 29(2)*: 157–163.

Auerswald, E. H. (1987). Epistemological confusion in family therapy and research. *Family Process, 26(3)*: 317–330.

Austin, J. L. (1976). *How to do things with words*. London: Oxford University Press.

Bandler, R., & Grinder, J. (1975). *The structure of magic*. Palo Alto, CA: Science & Behavior Books.

Bateson, G. (1972). Form, substance, and difference. In G. Bateson (Ed.), *Steps to an ecology of mind*. New York: Ballantine.

Bateson, G., Jackson, D. D., Haley, J., & Weakland, J. H. (1956). Toward a theory of schizophrenia. *Behavioral Science, 1*: 251–264.

Beels, C., & Ferber, A. (1973). What family therapists do. In A. Ferber, M. Mendelsohn, & A. Napier (Eds.), *The book of family therapy*. Boston: Houghton Mifflin.

Bloor, D. (1983). *Wittgenstein: A social theory of knowledge*. New York: Columbia University Press.

Bowen, M. (1966). The use of family theory in clinical practice. *Comprehensive Psychiatry, 7*: 345–374.

Cade, B. (1987). Brief/strategic approaches to therapy: A commentary. *Australian and New Zealand Journal of Family Therapy,* *8(1):* 37–44.

Capra, F. (1977). *The tao of physics.* New York: Bantam.

Carroll, L. (1972). *Alice's adventures in wonderland and through the looking-glass.* London: Tavistock.

Chomsky, N. (1968). *Language and mind.* New York: Harcourt, Bruce, Jovanovich.

Chomsky, N. (1980). *Rules and representations.* New York: Columbia University Press.

Cornille, T. (1989). Madanes presents 15 steps for dealing with sex abuse. *Family Therapy News,* November/December.

De Man, P. (1979). *Allegories of reading.* New Haven: Yale.

Derrida, J. (1978). *Writing and difference* (A. Bass, trans.). Chicago: University of Chicago Press.

Derrida, J. (1981). *Positions* (A. Bass, trans.). Chicago: University of Chicago Press.

de Shazer, S. (1974). On getting unstuck: Some change initiating tactics. *Family Therapy, 1(1):* 19–26.

de Shazer, S. (1975). Brief therapy: Two's company. *Family Process, 14:* 79–93.

de Shazer, S. (1982a). *Patterns of brief family therapy.* New York: Guilford.

de Shazer, S. (1982b). Some conceptual distinctions are more useful than others. *Family Process, 21:* 71–84.

de Shazer, S. (1984). The death of resistance. *Family Process, 23:* 79–93.

de Shazer, S. (1985). *Keys to solution in brief therapy.* New York: Norton.

de Shazer, S. (1988). *Clues: Investigating solutions in brief therapy.* New York: Norton.

de Shazer, S. (1989). Wrong map, wrong territory. *Journal of Marital and Family Therapy, 15(2):* 117–121.

de Shazer, S., & Berg, I. K. (1984). A part is not apart: Working with only one of the partners present. In A. Gurman (Ed.), *Casebook of marital therapy.* New York: Guilford.

de Shazer, S., Berg, I. K., Lipchik, E., Nunnally, E., Molnar, A., Gingerich, W. C., & Weiner-Davis, M. (1986). Brief therapy: Focused solution development. *Family Process, 25:* 207–221.

Dolan, Y. (1985). *A path with a heart: Ericksonian utilization with resistant and chronic clients.* New York: Brunner/Mazel.

Edwards, G., Orford, J., Egert, S., Guthrie, S., Hawker, A., Hensman, C., Mitcheson, M., Oppenheimer, E., & Taylor, C. (1977). Alcoholism: A controlled trial of "treatment" and "advice." *Journal of Studies on Alcohol, 38:* 1004–1031.

Epstein, N. B. (1988). Dilemmas and choices in the design of family therapy research. In L. C. Wynne, (Ed.), *The state of the art in family therapy research: Controversies and recommendations.* New York: Family Process Press.

Erickson, G. (1988). Against the grain: Decentering family therapy. *Journal of Marital and Family Therapy, 14(3)*: 225–236.

Erickson, M. H. (1954). Pseudo-orientation in time as a hypnotic procedure. *Journal of Clinical and Experiment Hypnosis, 2*: 261–283.

Family Therapy Networker. (1988, September/October). The constructivists are coming.

Fisch, R., Weakland, J. H., & Segal, L. (1983). *The tactics of change: Doing therapy briefly.* San Francisco: Jossey-Bass.

Fischer, H. R. (1987). 'Grammar' and 'language-game' as concepts for the analysis of schizophrenic communication. In R. Wodak & P. Van de Craen (Eds.), *Neurotic and psychotic language behavior.* Clevedon (U.K.): Multilingual Matters.

Fish, V. (1990). Introducing causality and power into family therapy theory: A correction to the systemic paradigm. *Journal of Marital and Family Therapy, 16(1)*: 21–37.

Fisher, S. (1980). The use of time limits in brief psychotherapy: A comparison of six-session, twelve session, and unlimited treatment of families. *Family Process, 19*: 377–392.

Fisher, S. (1984). Time-limited brief therapy with families: A one-year follow-up study. *Family Process, 23*: 101–106.

Foucault, M. (1972). History, discourse and discontinuity (A. Nazzaro, trans.). *Salmagundi, 20*: 229–33.

Freud, S. (1960). *Letters of Sigmund Freud,* (Edited by A. Freud). New York: Basic.

Gergen, K. J., & Gergen, M. J. (1983). Narratives of the self. In T. R. Sabin & K. E. Scheibe (Eds.), *Studies in social identity.* New York: Praeger.

Gergen, K. J., & Gergen, M. J. (1986). Narrative form and the construction of psychological science. In T. R. Sabin (Ed.), *Narrative psychology: The storied nature of human conduct.* New York: Praeger.

Giacomo, D., & Weissmark, M. (1987). Toward a generative theory of the therapeutic field. *Family Process, 26(3)*: 437–459.

Gingerich, W. C., de Shazer, S., & Weiner-Davis, M. (1988). Constructing change: A research view of interviewing. In E. Lipchik (Ed.), *Interviewing.* Rockville, MD: Aspen.

Goffman, E. (1974). *Frame analysis.* New York: Harper.

Gordan, D., & Meyers-Anderson, M. (1981). *Phoenix: Therapeutic patterns of Milton H. Erickson.* Cupertino, CA: Meta.

Gurman, A. (1988). Issues in the specification of family therapy interventions. In L. C. Wynne (Ed.), *The state of the art in family therapy research: Controversies and recommendations*. New York: Family Process Press.

Gustafson, J. P. (1986). *The complex secret of brief psychotherapy*. New York: Norton.

Haley, J. (1963). *Strategies of psychotherapy*. New York: Grune & Stratton.

Haley, J. (1967a). Toward a theory of pathological systems. In G. Zuk & I. Boszormenyi-Nagy (Eds.), *Family therapy and disturbed families*. Palo Alto, CA: Science & Behavior Books.

Haley, J. (Ed.). (1967b). *Advanced techniques of hypnosis and therapy*. New York: Grune & Stratton.

Haley, J. (1973). *Uncommon therapy*. New York: Norton.

Haley, J. (1987). *Problem-solving therapy* (2nd ed.). San Francisco: Jossey-Bass.

Hall, A., & Fagen, R. (1956). Definition of system. *General Systems Yearbook, 1*: 18–28.

Harland, R. (1987). *Superstructuralism: The philosophy of structuralism and post-structuralism*. London: Methuen.

Hintikka, M. B., & Hintikka, J. (1986). *Investigating Wittgenstein*. London: Basil Blackwell.

Hoffman, L. (1971). Deviation-amplifying processes in natural groups. In J. Haley (Ed.), *Changing families*. New York: Grune & Stratton.

Hoffman, L. (1981). *Foundations of family therapy: A conceptual framework for systems change*. New York: Basic.

Hoffman, L. (1990). Constructing realities: An art of lenses. *Family Process, 29(1)*: 1–12.

Jackson, D. D., & Weakland, J. H. (1961). Conjoint family therapy: Some considerations on theory, technique, and results. *Psychiatry, 24*: 30–45.

Kiser, D. (1988). *A follow-up study conducted at the Brief Family Therapy Center*. Unpublished manuscript.

Kiser, D., & Nunnally, E. (1990). *The relationship between treatment length and goal achievement in solution-focused therapy*. Unpublished manuscript.

Kuhn, T. (1970). *The structure of scientific revolutions* (2nd ed.). Chicago: University of Chicago Press.

Lange, A., & van der Hart, O. (1983). *Directive family therapy*. New York: Brunner/Mazel.

Langley, D., Pittman, F., Machotka, P., & Flomenhaft, K. (1968). Family crisis therapy — Results and implications. *Family Process, 7*: 145–158.

Lazarus, A., & Fay, A. (1990). Brief psychotherapy: Tautology or oxymoron. In J. Zeig & S. Gilligan (Eds.), *Brief therapy: Myths, methods, and metaphors*. New York: Brunner/Mazel.

Leitch, V. B. (1983). *Deconstructive criticism: An advanced introduction*. New York: Columbia University Press.

Levi-Strauss, C. (1963). *Structural anthropology*. New York: Basic Books.

Lincoln, Y. S., & Guba, E. G. (1985). *Naturalistic inquiry*. Beverly Hills: Sage.

Lipchik, E. (1988). Interviewing with a constructive ear. *Dulwich Centre Newsletter*, Winter, pp. 3–7.

Lyotard, Jean-François (1984). *The Postmodern condition: A report on Knowledge* (G. Bennington & B. Massumi, trans.). Minneapolis: University of Minnesota Press.

Malan, D. (1976). *The frontier of brief psychotherapy: An example of the convergence of research and clinical practice*. New York: Plenum.

Malan, D., Heath, S., Bascal, H., & Balfour, F. (1975). Psychodynamic changes in untreated neurotic patients. II. Apparently genuine improvements. *Archives of General Psychiatry, 32*: 110–126.

Mann, J. (1973). *Time-limited psychotherapy*. Cambridge, MA: Harvard University Press.

Maruyama, M. (1963). The second cybernetics: Deviation-amplifying mutual causal processes. *American Scientist, 5*: 164–179.

Maruyama, M. (1977). Heterogenistics: An epistemological restructuring of biological and social sciences. *Cybernetica, 20*: 69–86.

Maruyama, M. (1981). Personal communication.

Mehan, H., & Willis, J. (1988). MEND: A nurturing voice in the nuclear arms debate. *Social Problems, 35(4)*: 363–383.

Miller, G., & de Shazer, S. (1991). Jenseits von beschwerden: Ein entwurf kurztherapie (Beyond Complaints: A foundation for brief therapy). In L. Steiner & C. Ahlers (Eds.), *Systemic thinking and therapeutic process*. Heidelberg: Springer-Verlag.

Miller, J. H. (1976). Steven's rock and criticism as cure, II. *Georgia Review, 30*: 340–345.

Minuchin, S., Rosman, B., & Baker, L. (1978). *Psychosomatic families: Anorexia nervosa in context*. Cambridge, MA: Harvard.

Norris, C. (1983). *The deconstructive turn: Essays in the rhetoric of philosophy*. London: Methuen.

Norton, R. (1981). Soft magic. In C. Wilder & J. H. Weakland (Eds.), *Rigor & imagination: Essays from the legacy of Gregory Bateson*. New York: Praeger.

Nunnally, E., de Shazer, S., Lipchik, E., & Berg, I. K. (1986). A study of change: Therapeutic theory in process. In D. Efron (Ed.), *Journeys: Expansion of the strategic-systemic therapies*. New York: Brunner/Mazel.

O'Hanlon, W., & Weiner-Davis, M. (1989). *In search of solutions: A new direction in psychotherapy*. New York: Norton.

Orford, J., Oppenheimer, E., & Edwards, G. (1976). Abstinence or control: the outcome for excessive drinkers two years after consultation. *Behaviour Research and Therapy, 14*, 409–418.

Palazzoli, M., Boscolo, L., Cecchin, G., & Prata, G. (1978). *Paradox and counterparadox*. New York: Aronson.

Palazzoli, M., Cirillo, S., Selvini, M., & Sorrentino, A. (1989). *Family games: General models of psychotic processes in the family*. New York: Norton.

Papp, P. (1983). *The process of change*. New York: Guilford.

Paul, N. (1967). The role of mourning and empathy in conjoint marital therapy. In G. Zuk & I. Boszormenyi-Nagy (Eds.), *Family therapy and disturbed families*. Palo Alto, CA: Science & Behavior Books.

Pittman, F., Langsley, D., Flomenhaft, K., DeYoung, C., Machotka, P., & Kaplan, D. (1971). Therapy techniques of the family treatment unit. In J. Haley (Ed.), *Changing families*. New York: Grune & Stratton.

Sadler, J. Z., & Hulgus, Y. F. (1989). Hypothesizing and evidence-gathering: The nexus of understanding. *Family Process, 28(3)*: 255–267.

Sarup, M. (1989). *Post-structuralism and postmodernism*. Athens, GA: University of Georgia Press.

Scheflen, A. E. (1969a). Behavioral programs in human communication. In W. Gray, F. Duhl, & N. Rizzo (Eds.), *General systems theory and psychiatry*. Boston: Little, Brown.

Scheflen, A. E. (1969b). Systems and psychosomatics. In W. Gray, F. Duhl, & N. Rizzo (Eds.), *General systems theory and psychiatry*. Boston: Little, Brown.

Searle, J. R. (1970). *Speech acts: An essay in the philosophy of language*. London: Cambridge University Press.

Sifneos, P. (1965). Seven years' experience with short-term dynamic psychotherapy. 6th International Congress of Psychotherapy.

Sifneos, P. (1985). Short-term dynamic psychotherapy of phobic and mildly obsessive-compulsive patients. *American Journal of Psychotherapy, 39(3)*: 314–322.

Sifneos, P. (1990). Short-term anxiety-provoking psychotherapy (STAPP): Termination – outcome – and videotaping. In J. Zeig & S. Gilligan (Eds.), *Brief therapy: Myths, methods, and metaphors*. New York: Brunner/Mazel.

Simon, F., Stierlin, H., & Wynne, L. (1985). *The language of family therapy: A systemic vocabulary and sourcebook*. New York: Family Process Press.

Strupp, H. (1988). Personal communication.

Sluzki, C. (1988). Case commentary II. *Family Therapy Networker*, September/October, pp. 79–81.

Smith, C. S. (1978). Structural hierarchy in science, art, and history.

In J. Wechsler (Ed.), *On aesthetics in science*. Cambridge, MA: MIT Press.

Spencer-Brown, G. (1973). *Laws of form*. New York: Dutton.

Stanton, M. D. (1988). The lobster quadrille: Issues and dilemmas for family therapy research. In L. C. Wynne (Ed.), *The state of the art in family therapy research: Controversies and recommendations*. New York: Family Process Press.

Staten, H. (1984). *Wittgenstein and Derrida*. Lincoln, NE: University of Nebraska Press.

Stierlin, H. (1977). *Psychoanalysis & family therapy*. New York: Aronson.

Stierlin, H., & Weber, G. (1989). *Unlocking the family door: A systemic approach to the understanding and treatment of anorexia nervosa*. New York: Brunner/Mazel.

Talmon, M. (1990). *Single-session therapy*. San Francisco: Jossey-Bass.

Thom, R. (1975). *Structural stability and morphogenesis*. Reading, PA: Benjamin/Cummings.

Titchener, J. (1967). Family system as model for ego system. In G. Zuk & I. Boszormenyi-Nagy (Eds.), *Family therapy and disturbed families*. Palo Alto, CA: Science & Behavior Books.

Von Glasersfeld, E. (1984a). Steps in the construction of "others" and "reality": A study in self-regulation. Presented at the 7th European Meeting on Cybernetics and Systems Research: Vienna, Austria.

Von Glasersfeld, E. (1984b). An introduction to radical constructivism. In P. Watzlawick (Ed.), *The invented reality*. New York: Norton.

Watzlawick, P. (Ed.). (1984). *The invented reality*. New York: Norton.

Watzlawick, P., Beavin, J., & Jackson, D. D. (1967). *Pragmatics of human communication*. New York: Norton.

Watzlawick, P., & Weakland, J. H. (Eds.). (1977). *The interactional view*. New York: Norton.

Watzlawick, P., Weakland, J. H., & Fisch, R. (1974). *Change*. New York: Norton.

Weakland, J. H. (1982). 'Family Therapy' with individuals. Paper presented at the MRI/ETC Conference, Nice, France.

Weakland, J. H. (1990). Myths about brief therapy; Myths of brief therapy. In J. Zeig & S. Gilligan (Eds.), *Brief therapy: Myths, methods, and metaphors*. New York: Brunner/Mazel.

Weakland, J. H., Fisch, R., Watzlawick, P., & Bodin, A. (1974). Brief therapy: Focused problem resolution. *Family Process, 13*: 141–168.

Wechsler, J. (Ed.). (1978). *On aesthetics in science*. Cambridge, MA: MIT Press.

Weiner-Davis, M., de Shazer, S., & Gingerich, W. (1987). Using pretreatment change to construct a therapeutic solution: An exploratory study. *Journal of Marital and Family Therapy, 13(4)*: 359–363.

White, M. (1988). The process of questioning: A therapy of literary merit? *Dulwich Center Newsletter*, Winter, pp. 8–14.

Whitehead, A. N., & Russell, B. (1910). *Principia mathematica.* Cambridge (U.K.): University of Cambridge Press.

Wilden, A. (1980). *System and structure: Essays in communication and exchange* (2nd ed.). London: Tavistock.

Wittgenstein, L. (1958). *The blue and brown books.* New York: Harper & Row.

Wittgenstein, L. (1968). *Philosophical investigations* (G. E. M. Anscombe, trans.) (3rd Ed.). New York: Macmillan.

Wittgenstein, L. (1975a). *Philosophical remarks* (R. Hargreaves & R. White, trans.). Chicago: University of Chicago Press.

Wittgenstein, L. (1975b). *Philosophical grammar.* Oxford: Blackwell.

Wittgenstein, L. (1980). *Culture and value* (P. Winch, trans.). Chicago: University of Chicago Press.

Wynne, L. (1971). Some guidelines for exploratory conjoint family therapy. In J. Haley (Ed.), *Changing families.* New York: Grune & Stratton.

Zuk, G. (1967). Family therapy. *Archives of General Psychiatry, 16*: 71–79.

Zweben, A., Pearlman, S., & Li, S. (1988). A comparison of brief advice and conjoint therapy in the treatment of alcohol abuse: The results of the marital systems study. *British Journal of Addiction, 83*: 899–916.

NAME INDEX

SUBJECT INDEX

177